"RC Shaw embarks on a saltwater adventure as impressive and extreme as they come. The author and renowned surfer weaves a profoundly moving travelogue that will entertain, impress, inspire, and uplift. Sailors, sea lovers, and Maritimers will devour this story as readily as anyone who enjoys a tale of overcoming the odds and rising up in the face of adversity. Funny, thought-provoking, entertaining, and magnetically written, *Captain Solitude* is an essential read. You will ride the waves with Shaw on every page."

— James Mullinger, author of *Brit Happens*

"Who hasn't wanted to travel by bicycle along gravel back roads, jumping into the ocean whenever the mood strikes? (Okay, maybe just RC Shaw and I.) Shaw survives his great Maritime journey with stops at farmers markets, gas stations, deserted beaches, and a surprising number of graveyards. Describing the South Shore and the people who live there, *Captain Solitude* makes a strong case for why all of us should push ourselves beyond our respective comfort zones and reminds us that true self-discovery is never found through a self-help book or a meditation app but in the depths of the unknown and in the unending gifts we receive from the Earth and the kindness of its people."

— Afie Jurvanen (Bahamas)

"Adventure has become an increasingly lost art, even though the world is riper than ever for exploration. Children, work, danger, and utter hassle rule. Shaw's *Captain Solitude* not only inspires but resets addled minds. His quest to explore, to adventure, to live again is an inspiration that must be devoured. The prose is taut, the mission clean. Most importantly, though, the ideal of living bigger resounds. Now more than ever. Essential."

— Chas Smith, author of *Welcome to Paradise, Now Go to Hell*

Also by RC Shaw

Louisbourg or Bust

CAPTAIN

One Surfer's Search for
the World's Greatest Sailor

SOLITUDE

RC SHAW

GOOSE LANE

Edited by James Langer.
Copy edited by Paula Sarson.
Cover and page design by Julie Scriver.
Cover illustration by Julie Scriver with inspiration from Uehara Konen.
Map by Jeffrey C. Domm.
Printed in Canada by Marquis.
10 9 8 7 6 5 4 3 2 1

Library and Archives Canada Cataloguing in Publication

Title: Captain solitude : one surfer's search for the world's greatest sailor / RC Shaw.
Names: Shaw, R. C., 1978- author.

Identifiers: Canadiana (print) 2023056822X | Canadiana (ebook) 20230568262 |
ISBN 9781773103303 (softcover) | ISBN 9781773103310 (EPUB) | ISBN 9781773103303

Subjects: LCSH: Shaw, R. C., 1978-—Travel—Nova Scotia. | LCSH: Slocum, Joshua, 1844-1909—
Homes and haunts—Nova Scotia—Brier Island. | LCSH: Cycling—Nova Scotia.|
LCSH: Brier Island (N.S.)—Description and travel. | LCSH: Nova Scotia—Description and travel.

Classification: LCC FC2317.6 .S49 2024 | DDC 917.16/2045—dc23

Goose Lane Editions acknowledges the generous support of the Government of Canada, the Canada Council for the Arts, and the Government of New Brunswick.

Goose Lane Editions is located on the unceded territory of the Wəlastəkwiyik whose ancestors along with the Mi'kmaq and Peskotomuhkati Nations signed Peace and Friendship Treaties with the British Crown in the 1700s.

Goose Lane Editions
500 Beaverbrook Court, Suite 330
Fredericton, New Brunswick
CANADA E3B 5X4
gooselane.com

MIX
Paper from
responsible sources
FSC® C103567

In memory of Neal Durling

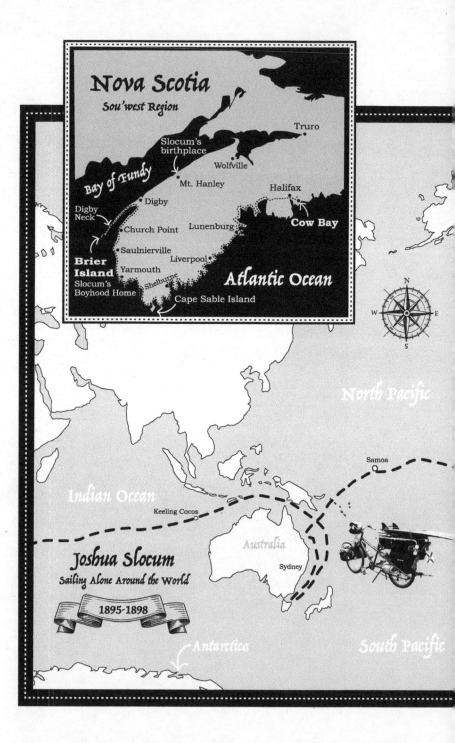

Nova Scotia
Sou'west Region

Truro

Slocum's birthplace

Wolfville

Bay of Fundy

Mt. Hanley

Halifax

Digby

Cow Bay

Digby Neck

Church Point

Lunenburg

Saulnierville

Liverpool

Brier Island

Yarmouth

Slocum's Boyhood Home

Shelburne

Cape Sable Island

Atlantic Ocean

North Pacific

Samoa

Indian Ocean

Keeling Cocos

Australia

Sydney

Joshua Slocum
Sailing Alone Around the World
1895-1898

Antarctica

South Pacific

N
W — E
S

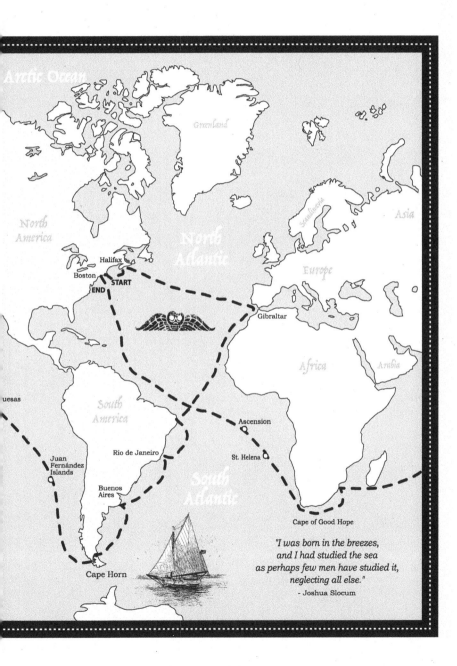

"I was born in the breezes,
and I had studied the sea
as perhaps few men have studied it,
neglecting all else."
- Joshua Slocum

PART ONE

ROCKBOUND

Chapter 1

SHAKEDOWN

He had fear in his heart, but gloried in the fury of the gale.
— *Rockbound*

It was the first day of school, and I wasn't going. As our sensible minivan crunched down the gravel and straightened for the road, I flailed like one of those inflatable tube men, blowing kisses and miming hugs to Genny and the girls as they waved back. Then they were gone.

For a minute, my highly structured teacher-dad-husband brain swirled with frantic energy, spinning up a smoothie of domestic concerns and renegade emotions. Did they pack enough to eat? Will they make new friends? Could my students forget me? Am I a selfish fool?

The grey Atlantic horizon offered no answers, but its ruler-straight line drew my eye and slowed my breath. One-hundred-and-twenty-six years earlier, a bald fifty-one-year-old man in a three-piece suit would have a been a speck on that line, a lone sailor turning east on the sailboat he built himself, the lights of Halifax Harbour the last North American beacons he'd see for three full years. Joshua Slocum, Nova Scotia's saltiest son and the world's greatest sailor. My dude. I could almost sense him out there, all alone, knifing through the chop.

And here's where I should ratchet up my reason for stepping away from teaching to undertake some mid-life transformation, the more radical the better. I'm forty-four years old, the perfect age to embody a cliché. Ripe for all kinds of crisis. But I can't fudge it. My marriage is rock-solid, I love my kids, I like my job, and I live within walking distance of a headland that can, on occasion, produce clean waves that serve up almond-shaped slots to slip through. On the surface, I'm as conflicted as a cat curled up next to a wood stove.

Problem is, I have an obsession, an itch I've been meticulously planning to scratch for the same duration as Slocum's unthinkable odyssey. Moments after I closed *Sailing Alone Around the World*, his classic book, my mind hatched its own quest. A stunt really. A no-phone, no-tech, leg-powered lark. This was my vision: I would stuff my cargo bike with camping gear and pedal solo from my driveway in Cow Bay to distant Brier Island, Nova Scotia's most southwesterly point and Joshua Slocum's boyhood home. Why? Three burning reasons: to surf uncharted waves, to experience deep solitude, and to crack a mystery no seabound scholar has ever solved—what happened to Joshua Slocum when he disappeared nine years after circumnavigating the globe?

As the first drops of sky spittle found my face, I knew I had to snap out of it and start moving. I was about to do what only a sailing virgin would do: leave in a storm. A Hurricane Ida–strength gale to be exact.

In my mind, this departure date was immovable. When else would a teacher get to embark on a September voyage of adventure that didn't involve emailing, photocopying, laminating, border-stapling, and seating-plan creation?

So when Hurricane Ida crossed the Bay of Fundy after testing the dykes of New Orleans a week earlier and tracked, against my fervid prayers, toward Nova Scotia, I kept my schedule inked. If I'd known what awaited me, I would have been a smart sailor and held off a day.

My cargo bike looked ready though. I circled it in the mist, checking for snugness. I had everything I would need. Borrowed waterproof front panniers with clothes, tools, bags of nuts and dried mango. Dry bag backpack with sleeping bag, poncho, and wetsuit. A newly acquired, and soon-to-be nemesis, hammock tent locked and loaded on the bench seat. Front handlebar box with notebook, camera, Grandpa's pipe, ripped-out road maps, and a topped-up flask of Teacher's malt whisky.

Four-litre bottle of water and snorkel kit lashed on either side of the back wheel frame. Essential weird stuff like Chicken Tender (my red Penny skateboard), black awooga trumpet horn with wine-cork mute, and stone-dead 1950s Westclox clock zip-tied to the handlebars, of course.

To max out the weirdness, I had my Conjuring Kit. Joshua Slocum had been gone for a century, so I reckoned I'd have to find other ways to reach him. There was my Magic 8 Ball, cradled to the frame in a homemade bicycle tube sling; a Death tarot card, tucked away in my notebook; and the wooden staff I'd borrowed from the abandoned birth house of Slocum himself, in Mount Hanley, an object I believed he may once have touched.

Then there were the books. I'd packed Frank Parker Day's *Rockbound*, Helen Creighton's *Bluenose Ghosts*, and a pocket edition of Slocum's magnum opus — two inches by three — so it would literally never leave my side.

And just one more thing. The kit's topper, my most crucial piece of cargo, a black 5'2" twin-fin Mini Simmons surfboard shaped by a friend for the journey, a wave-riding slab we dubbed the Tombstone. There it was, lashed tight by two bungees, its shark fins flanking the seat, giving the whole set-up a slapdash Batmobile effect.

If the dark stars aligned, these talismans would come together, Voltron-like, to produce ... well, if not an answer, then at least a wild story.

I strapped on my beat-up black helmet and mounted the metal beast. Instantly strained forearms told me it weighed substantially north of a hundred pounds, a face slap to my vow of packing light. I shook my head, muscled into balance, and pushed forward off the industrial-strength kickstand.

After a merciful downhill to the main road, I turned south past the white oceanside church that stands at the heart of our four hundred strong community, a quietly eccentric surf burg on the ragged edge of the North Atlantic. A compost truck blocked my path, replacing the briny seaweed air with a less traditionally maritime scent. I scrunched up my nose and followed it across the causeway, past our famous moose statue and south into Eastern Passage, Cow Bay's bigger and more densely populated cousin, where the hottest news of the previous year was the addition of our very own A&W.

As I hit the busy Woodside commuter road, the drizzle increased, and I felt my knees begin to resist the piston-like action I was subjecting them to. *Forward*, I thought, *only forward*.

Combustion rules the roost on this stretch of asphalt, so I was extra thankful to make the Dartmouth bike path in one piece. After a snaky harbourside roll, where I tested my muffled horn on a few surprised pedestrians, I merged back onto the road to tackle the sweeping incline that leads to the Macdonald Bridge bike lane into Halifax. There I stopped to catch my heaving breath and take a squirt from my water bottle in the rain.

Both Halifax Harbour bridges offer up sweeping views, but the "old bridge," as the Macdonald is known to locals, is the only one you can bike across. I looked north first, taking in The Narrows with its flank of east coast navy vessels and giant shipbuilding dockyards, the "new" MacKay Bridge, and beyond that the expansive spoon-shaped Bedford Basin, its rim dotted with houses and apartment buildings.

To the south I spied forested McNabs Island and the rocky crags of Chebucto Head framing the harbour mouth. I scanned the Dartmouth waterfront with its enormous Canada flag flying over a clutch of office buildings, then watched the public ferry chug past tiny Georges Island. I swept my gaze across Halifax's storied downtown to the hive of distant container ship cranes, back along the bustling docks, and up the gauntlet of mini skyscrapers to its partially obscured Citadel Hill, the city's bastion-turned-tourist-mecca.

This was The City, as it's known in every Nova Scotian town outside commuting distance. The city I fell in love with as a twenty-six-year-old after a long, awestruck ramble in its old burial grounds on Barrington Street. The city that ushered us into a sight-unseen, mouse-infested apartment above a Thai restaurant. The city where, after a visit to the neighbouring hostel's job board, I decided I would become a working sailor on a bona fide tall ship.

Tall Ship Silva is best known as a booze cruiser, a uniquely Haligonian floating patio. Her towering masts are mainstays on the waterfront vista, and hordes of summer tourists flock to the vessel for her affordable harbour tour. I've watched many a mariner eye the *Silva* and scratch their heads. Her black steel hull appears indestructible, exuding a barge-like practicality that clashes with her five heavy-duty white sails.

And it's true, the *Silva* is unique. Built in 1939 in Sweden, her 130-foot schooner rig was the last of a series of seven "motor sailors" added to the Swedish merchant marine's fleet, built in response to a shortage of bunker fuel in the Baltic Sea. After running supplies in the war years, the MV *Silva* became an important coal carrier, so important that when she sank in fifty metres of water she was immediately salvaged, spruced up, and put back to work. Function, reliability, sheer mass — the *Silva* has never won any beauty awards.

"Y'have any boating experience?" the bearded captain asked me one morning on the wharf next to the resting *Silva*. His eyes were bloodshot, and I could see his hands quivering around his travel mug.

"Oh ya," I said, "of course. I've been on lots of boats."

Either he was still half asleep or just desperate, but he neglected to ask the key follow-up that would call me out: Any *sailing* experience? I wasn't prepared to lie, so luckily I didn't have to.

I got the deckhand job right then and there. In truth, every boat I'd ever handled was a tiny craft with tiny motors on tiny inland lakes. But I was confident that my apprenticeship with outboard engines and my growing surf skills would be enough to help me fake it till I made it.

After my first shift, where I fumbled with everything, yanked the wrong ropes, and showed a dearth of knowledge around any knot but the one I tied my shoes with, the captain came down to the ship's cabin, where the crew was enjoying a post-cruise courtesy beer. He called me up to the deck.

"Here, young man," he said in a gruff voice. He wasn't jittery anymore, having drained the contents of his morning mug. He passed me a cigar-shaped microphone, yanking at its coil with his free hand.

Confused, I took the mic.

"You seem like the type to tell a story. None of the other deckhands wanna do it, so I need you to be our commentator."

Commentator? The annoying tour guide that most passengers tuned out? *That* guy?

"Uhh…," I said, "I, uh, well I just moved here. I don't know any of the history." I swung my arm across the harbour's expanse. "Like, I don't even know what that island's called."

"That's Georges Island, mate," he said, flashing me a pirate's smirk. "You'll figure it out. Take these home this weekend and read 'em both. Scan 'em at least."

He grabbed two books from behind a bench and slapped them in my palm. Looking back, it was a kind of sacrament, a holy initiation into Joshua Slocum's realm, but at the time it felt more like a homework assignment.

"First one," he said, jabbing the top book, "that's your history. Read it for the stories you'll have to tell: the Halifax Explosion, harbour defence over the years—the Citadel, McNabs, the other forts—the VE Day Riots, and George's prison island of course."

The book was *Halifax: Warden of the North* by Thomas H. Raddall, a legendary Nova Scotian I'd never heard of.

"And this one," he said, flipping the other book over, "that's to get ya thinkin' about what it means to be a true Bluenose sailor. It's a good yarn. Great for workin' up yer east coast accent too."

"*Rockbound*," I whispered. The cover had a close-up of a white-bearded, blue-eyed old salt in a bright yellow, rain-soaked sou'wester. His hand clutched a weathered rope. It was Captain Highliner and he was staring into my soul.

"The Classic Novel of Nova Scotia's South Shore?" I read out, meeting the captain's squint.

"Just a label they added later on. Kinda right, though," he mused. "Look at 'em this weekend, eh?"

He didn't wait for my response. When I went back down to the cabin, my new crewmates were grinning.

"Looks like we got our microphone man!" one guy called out. Everyone cracked up. I just stood there with the books cradled in my armpit, a running back with no idea where the end zone was.

Luckily I loved to read, and I burned through both before my next shift. *Halifax: Warden of the North* was a mainline injection of local lore. *Rockbound* was another beast entirely, a fictional tale set in a region that was pure myth to me at the time. I remember one scene stopped me in my tracks: protagonist David Jung, alone on a wooden sailboat, deftly adjusting his sails to harness the changing wind. I had no idea a person could sail solo. To me, sailing was a dozen athletes in Oakley sunglasses perched on the rail of a sleek racing yacht, doing whatever they did to win the trophy. *Rockbound* showed me something new. It was a key I stashed away, a key I would need to open an unknown, future lock.

When I saw the *Silva* packed with American tourists fresh off a massive Carnival cruise boat, I took the mic with a touch of confidence and launched into the history of McNabs Island, pointing out the exact spot where sailors disloyal to the British Crown were hanged as a reminder to newcomers to behave. *This is fresh history*, I thought. So fresh to me that I just learned it yesterday!

The Americans ate it up though, and I took to studying the names of college sports teams so I could break the ice with a call of "Go Hawkeyes!" whenever I saw someone in an "Iowa" sweater. I even got some cash tips, the value of which seemed to correlate with the number of football teams I pretended to know.

I had the job no one else wanted, but I didn't mind it. Only years later did I realize that instead of becoming a sailor, I had taken a firm step on the road to school teaching.

For the two months I talked myself hoarse on the *Silva*, she never ran on sail power alone. Technically, she didn't sail at all. Her loud, stanky, oil-slicked diesel engine was her sole propulsion. The "sailing" tourists were oblivious; the deckhands made a big production of it, but they only raised and lowered her sails for show.

A rude gust of wet wind woke me from my reverie as I sat there, straddling my wheeled load, which I was already calling the Ox. The bridge shuddered and swung, making me feel as if I were adrift on the open ocean. "Onward?" I said, slipping my flip-flops back into the pedal baskets. By then I was nearly soaked, but I'd prepared by wearing board shorts and lashing a pair of kid swim goggles on my helmet, just in case.

The only way off Macdonald Bridge on bicycle, incredibly, is to follow a corkscrewing, fenced-in path that slings you into warp speed and spits you out on perilous Barrington Street, the downtown artery that's more highway than residential road.

I clicked through my trusty seven gears and found the limit immediately, forced to coast along in the right lane while cars and transit buses threw rainwater rooster tails at me. The only respite was the lovely separated bike lane on Hollis Street, which I laboured on, up to Morris Street, the uphill straight shot to our school behind Dalhousie University.

I took Morris for nostalgic reasons. This was our route when the girls were small enough to both fit on the bike's bench seat, their backpacks wedged as cushions, giggling and cheering me on with a chorus of "Go Daddy go!" as I inched us up the same steep climb. To make our crazy commute work, we'd load the cargo bike in the van, race from Cow Bay to the Woodside ferry, unload and shunt the whole gear hurricane down two flights of stairs, ride the ferry with our helmets on, roll off, and mount our Dad-powered family steed. Of course, kids grow, as I feared they would, and the bike's function as a three-person rickshaw faded away. Act Two, as the Ox, had arrived.

Near the top of Dalhousie's campus, I swung wide and came around to Oxford Street with a direct view of our school, the building I'd laughed and cried and marked and marked and marked in for the past decade and a half. I had thought this would be the ultimate teacher fantasy: commute to school on the first day and, instead of tucking in the proverbial shirt and morphing into Mr. Shaw, pedal my surf-camping monstrosity right by, headed for a mental landscape devoid of bells and homework checks and playground duty and copier jams and innumerable Google Docs, into a phoneless expanse of unscheduled solitude.

As I rolled past, I was surprised at my melancholy. Sure, freewheeling solo adventure awaited. But I was leaving a part of my identity behind, and I knew all those teacher-student diamond moments — that rare, precious resource — would be stillborn, gone before they even happened.

By a stroke of luck, two notoriously late Grade 10 students I'd started a skateboard club with the previous year caught sight of me.

"Hey, Mr. Shaw!" the louder guy called out.

"Hi!" I yelled back.

They looked confused.

"You coming to school?"

"Nope," I said. "No, I'm heading to Brier Island, searching for the ghost of Joshua Slocum."

They both looked at each other, as if this news didn't compute. I'd kept my sabbatical plan hush-hush to prevent the rumour mill from grinding my gears. They shrugged in unison, and the quieter guy gave me a crisp, goofy salute.

And that was it; the sour taste in my mouth was gone. I knew they'd be just fine. The school would continue to energize and educate, with or without me. I was free. Maybe if I leaned hard enough into it, I'd return with something fresh to offer.

It teemed rain as I merged onto the Armdale roundabout and pedalled as hard as I could. The traffic circle was navigable, but the snaking St. Margarets Bay Road that led away was a cruel, uphill monster. As the chain of cars whipped past, I vowed to find the mythical Rum Runners Trail, a 119-kilometre path converted from an old rail line that once connected Halifax to Lunenburg. In my hard-core, pre-trip planning mind, this would have to be skipped because of its convenient, all-too-easy flatness. Fear-for-your-life road cycling has a way of lowering bars.

After nearly merging onto the main highway in the teeth of a Hurricane Ida headwind, I got desperate and pulled into a hotel parking lot. I docked the Ox and stepped through the automatic sliding doors into an eerily quiet and dry lobby. The woman at the front desk stated the obvious — "You're wet!" — and told me how I'd find the trail.

"Once more unto the breach!" I said as I stepped back into the maelstrom. An elderly couple unloading their car gave me a quizzical glance. Couldn't they recognize this as an adventure of a lifetime? No, no they could not. To them, I was an odd fellow with unfathomable motives, motives I myself had temporarily forgotten. This wasn't fun, I realized. This was wet and difficult.

The gale peaked as I turned from soulless Bayers Lake Business Park onto the smooth asphalt of the trail. Though I'd never been wetter in my life, and though the wind gusts seemed to come from under me somehow, entering the deserted trail brought a sense of safety that allowed my tense body to relax in an instant. My legs turned to noodles, my wrists uncoiled ropes. I slowed down to walking speed and glided on, mesmerized by the line of water spouting off the Ox's front tire directly at my shorts. All around me goldfinches and sparrows dipped and zipped, brushy squirrels darted across the trail, and I caught sight of the agitated waters of a rocky lake fringed by ash trees, each one a firework of gyrating yellow leaves. For fanfare, I squeaked my horn three times in the squall and made sure to yell, "See ya later, Halifax!" loud enough for my new best friends, the woodland creatures of the trail, to hear.

I found the right gear and kept grinding. As the trail changed from asphalt to crusher dust, the landscape became wetland bog, and soon I was surrounded by gnarled tamarack trees and ruby-red pitcher plants. I forged into the sheets of rain until the trail became a tunnel of elms that cut the wind and gave me false hope that the storm was on its last legs. Not so much. At the Bike & Bean Café, a sweet little train station turned bike/caffeine shop, I sipped a coffee and watched the Ox quaver in the wind, water shedding off the Tombstone in steady rivulets. The café clock told me it was getting on mid-afternoon, so I had to make my first of one million decisions on my voyage: tent in the rain—my initial, naïve plan—or shoot for a friend's barn in French Village, about five kilometres away on a busy road with no shoulder.

"Magic 8 Ball time," I whispered.

For the youngsters out there who have never had the bizarre fortune to put their decision-making faith in the hands of the greatest twentieth-century fad, here's a description. Picture a black billiard ball, make it plastic, enlarge it to grapefruit-size, fill it with mystical liquid (water plus blue dye), insert a couple of pyramid-shaped dice with unique responses on each face (from the ecstatic *Yes Definitely* to the heart-rending *Outlook Not Good*), add a transparent round plastic porthole, and there you have it. Your very own oracle. Gently shake, turn, and wait for an answer to float up.

A word to the wise, however: try to keep your questions as inconsequential as you can. Asking "Will I ever fall in love?" might be a tad heavy for your backpack Nostradamus. Stick to questions that have little chance of pulling you into an existential spiral.

Back in the rain, I reached down and gingerly tugged the orb from its rubber cradle. I sloshed it around and focused on the 8.

"Should I go for the barn instead of the hammock tent tonight?" I asked out loud, concentrating hard on the question.

I turned it over and watched the ghostly white pyramids jostle in the blue deeps, one face floating up to press itself into view.

It Is Certain

"Oooh," I gasped, "barn it is then!" And that was that.

Peggys Cove Road had everything the trail did not, namely large metal combustion boxes travelling at alarming speeds in proximity to the Ox and I. It also had hills. As I came into the full force of a hair-blower headwind, I clicked my brain to robot mode. "The white line is mine" became my mantra as I pedalled along, wary of the unpredictable pockmarked gravel strip to my right. Only once did I hit the ditch, frantically trying to yank my feet from their pedal baskets before I heaved over into the rocky bullrush steeps. Once was enough though. By the time I got to the barn, my face felt twisted by a grimace of fear.

No one was around, so I pushed the Ox up the grassy slope to the faded red barn, swung the heavy doors open, and let myself in. A dry place! What a miracle. Already I was feeling thankful for the small stuff.

After I guided the Ox over the creaky floorboards, I took my time and stripped him completely, laying everything out on a dusty workbench for inspection. The waterproof bags had worked their magic. This was the end of my *shakedown* day, a word the *Sailing Bible* defines as "an initial trip with a boat [or bike!] to make sure everything is operating properly." At first glance, all looked well.

As the afternoon flowed by, the rain quit and I knew an ocean swim had to happen. I grabbed my towel and my copy of *Rockbound* and hobbled across the road to the dock just in time to see the sun bust through a wall of indigo cloud and illuminate the small horseshoe bay inside the bigger bay they call St. Margarets.

"Blessed by the saint herself," I said in my best preacher impression.

I flattened out, starfish-style, on the warming wood. I'm not much of a yoga guy, but my body cried out for long pretzel stretches, spontaneous positions I'm sure have never been attempted before. A bystander would probably call the paramedics if they saw me, fearing I was in the grips of paralysis. By the end of it, I was face down on my towel, too overwhelmed by my body's voltage to move.

I took a deep breath, cleared my thoughts, and stood up.

The bay bristled with sailboats. I couldn't separate a sloop from a yawl from a dory, but I knew they were proper sailboats, not impostors like the diesel-guzzling *Tall Ship Silva*.

These vessels bobbed at anchor, masts bare and standing tall, looking a lot like Joshua Slocum's *Spray*.

I'd arrived. This was the South Shore.

As my toes gripped the dock's edge, I stared at the water and murmured a silent wish to get out there, at least once, under the rippling sheets of a real sailboat. Didn't Slocum's spirit demand it? How else could I get inside that mysterious, bald head of his? Then I exhaled and dove, straight down, into the bright blue darkness.

Chapter 2

HANG-UPS

Time never stood still, but flowed by him
like the tide through Sou'west gutter.
—— *Rockbound*

In *Rockbound*, Frank Parker Day's 1928 novel, David is David but Goliath is subbed out for Uriah, a harsh old-time fisherman with a potty mouth and an insatiable appetite for wealth and power. Underdog David Jung is our hero. Orphaned at a young age, he's left to his own devices and raised by a taskmaster drunk of a stepfather, who treats him more like a punching bag than a son. The book opens with eighteen-year-old David rowing his battered dory from Big Outpost Island to Rockbound Island, where Uriah—his great-uncle and "rich king of Rockbound"—runs the show.

Fate is a thunderhead theme, casting lightning bolts of destiny down on David at regular intervals. As he rows toward Rockbound and a confrontation with Uriah, he stops for a slack tide rest and asks the universe for a sign. An offshore breeze crops up in response, pushing him in the saddle-shaped island's direction.

Everyone knows an interloper has arrived the instant David lands on Rockbound, and gruff Uriah immediately tells him to get lost. David, a muscular lad with hair on his chest, plays the ace up his sleeve. He's recently learned that his family connection through his grandfather—Uriah's brother—guarantees him ownership of a tenth of the island, a little slice of land with a derelict house that Uriah has commandeered as storage for lobster traps. Uriah grudgingly concedes and agrees to give David a month's trial of fishing alongside his three burly sons.

The gods smile on David the very next day, when he out-sails and out-fishes everyone, returning loaded to the gunwales with cod. David knows the cold shoulders he receives are a Rockbounder's greatest compliment. As he says, "I sticks and I stays." Cue the epic battle of wills.

As I backtracked to Highway 3 from French Village in the chill of a clouded morning, I focused my fuzzy crosshairs on East Ironbound Island, the one Frank Parker Day modelled *Rockbound* on. My ripped-out map confirmed it was due south of the Aspotogan Peninsula and due east of Big and Little Tancook Islands. With no way to reach it, I knew my best bet for psychic connection was to camp within view and just sit there and stare at the island, for hours if necessary.

The Ox was keen to work, I could tell. After my gear shakedown and a solid semi-drying, everything felt snug behind me, and I found I could reach back and straighten the Tombstone with one hand while steering with the other. Sure, the Ox was heavy—maybe rotund is the right word?—but its sheer mass was a gift on the downhills that, if I tricked myself, could overcome the anchor-like effect it had on each hellacious ascent.

Back on the Rum Runners Trail, I quickly forgot about hills and locked into a slow and steady pace, a daydreamy rhythm enhanced by the Narnia-evoking foliage tunnel around me.

It was a twenty-kilometre roll from Upper Tantallon to Hubbards, where I hoped to have my first roadside meal. Head of St. Margarets Bay, Boutiliers Point, Ingramport, Black Point, all dots on my map that I snuck past on the grey line that runs like a stitched gash along the coastline. Though it was quiet, I did come across other humans on the trail, a nice change from my previous rain run.

One dude in particular got me thinking about my unsafe goal of being a stealthy, dark, near-invisible cyclist. I made out his lighthouse-bright beam first, and as he came toward me, I was swept up by a strange feeling of time travel. He seemed to be flying through space, a grinning juggernaut in a neon yellow safety vest and overly tight shorts, rocking a svelte aerated helmet with a tiny tentacle-style rear-view mirror, topped off with reflective glasses that lent him an air of a cyborg on ecstasy.

He *ch-chinged* his bell as he flew past, somehow barely pedalling, and I noticed his bike's frame seemed bulked up between his legs. I risked a confused look back. Maybe this *was* a magic forest, I thought, a place where alchemy rules. Wait, nope, I wasn't speeding up or even holding pace, I was grounding to a halt. That's when the penny dropped, and I realized he was riding an e-bike. Electric assist! Like biking but without all that pesky effort. Genius. I'd heard about them but hadn't seen one in the wild yet. Was it too late to modify the Ox? Yes, yes it was. My way would be the hard way.

By the time I found the gravel off-ramp to Hubbards, a beachy sailing village home to the Hooked Rug Museum of North America and legendary kitchen-party roadhouse the Shore Club, I was consumed by hunger. Quick rain droplets raked me as I scanned the main drag for a restaurant, any restaurant that might serve up the goods. A sandwich board outside the Trellis Café forced me hard on the handbrakes. They had burgers, the handmade kind. After planting the Ox under an awning, I grabbed my notebook and maps and entered the nearly empty spot, nodding to the few locals on my way to the leafy patio.

After ordering the burger and downing a glass of ice water, I decided to take some notes on my state of anticipation. Words like *excited* and *stoked* and *famished* seasoned the page as I worked to fill the pre-burger time and distract my stomach. When the server brought my plate, I snapped out of my trance as if she'd woken me from a nap. Weird customer alert. Of course I was effusive in thanking her for delivering what I now consider to be the World's Greatest Burger.

Maybe it was the circumstances — everything tastes better after physical exertion — or maybe stacking the burger up against my previous meal was unfair — handfuls of gorp and dried mango — or maybe, and I choose to believe this, the burger was made by God herself. I know I will never have a better first bite than that one.

Thankfully I was alone, because I was making noise, lots of it. I savoured each bite of perfectly spiced meat with its perfect condiment sidekicks and perfect bun, and I made sure to chew as slowly as my jaws would allow. The poor home fries sat neglected as I directed my whole soul at the burger.

"How's it taste?" a voice from the ether said. I looked up and there was the server, jug of ice water in hand.

"If I could hug the chef, I would."

"Oh," she laughed, "that's nice! I'll let her know you like it."

"No," I said, suddenly serious, "please tell her that I love it, *love* it. This burger is changing my life."

She laughed again, searching for the jest in my voice, and she took an extra moment to collect herself when she realized I was speaking in absolute earnest.

After I paid my bill, I passed through the café in a daze. A woman smiled at me from the kitchen. No words were exchanged, but I lifted my eyebrows in her direction, mouthing the word "you?" to which she threw back a head nod. My hands instinctively shot up into a prayer of thanks position, and I even bowed. If ever there was a holy burger, it can be found at the Trellis Café in Hubbards, Nova Scotia.

As the sun showers gave way to a sky pierced by occasional shafts of light, I turned the Ox onto Route 329, my mind and body charged up. The fabled Aspotogan loop lay ahead, one of the most respected cycling routes in the province and a road I'd never taken before.

Within ten minutes, I was walking the Ox up a nasty hill, my stomach flashing with cramps. A man in a little white house at the top gave me a polite wave, and I tried to smile back through my cavernous breaths.

"Tough one, that," he said.

"My kingdom for an e-bike!" I gasped in response. We both laughed.

Just beyond Bayswater, I pulled into the Swissair Flight 111 Memorial site for a rest and came face to face with a tragedy that rocked the communities of St. Margarets Bay in the overnight hours of September 2, 1998.

That night, the slate-grey Atlantic claimed 229 lives. A silent pall came over me as I read the names etched into the wall and realized that whole families had been lost on the flight from New York bound for Geneva. Victims' remains are interred here in a circle fenced off by granite headstones connected by chain. A still place. A place to pause and give thanks for existence. A place to steel yourself against random tragedy. The urge to see Genny and the girls was overpowering.

Sombre thoughts, digested with a generous helping of sea air, tend to flower into gratitude for me. Death is always right there, so every moment of consciousness on this side of the veil should be treated as a gift, right? And death needs to be acknowledged once in a while; death needs to be waltzed with. Otherwise it's just a ghastly void that scares the pants off us every time we think about it. Like Dumbledore says in J.K. Rowling's *Harry Potter and the Half-Blood Prince*, "It is the unknown we fear when we look upon death and darkness, nothing more."

As I pedalled away from the memorial site, I realized that my solo adventure would give me ample time to ruminate on what happens after life ends. I had the uncanny feeling that finding Slocum depended on it.

Near the tip of the Aspotogan Peninsula sits Bayswater Beach, a white-sand gem facing open ocean, and I held some hope that it might be showing swell. Not so much. It was pancake flat, so I kept my Tombstone sheathed, promising myself I'd get in the water soon, even if just for a paddle.

I had to find an incognito spot to pitch my spanking new hammock tent, the romantic purchase I had made on the recommendation of a few intrepid buds who swore by it. After crossing a thickly forested inland road, I came to a *Dead End* sign and followed it up and away from the main route, digging deep as I passed the tidy houses and fragrant apple trees lining New Harbour Road. I tried my best to ignore a rabid German shepherd taking ghost runs at me before hitting the end of his tether and jerking upward—a hell-hound if I'd ever seen one—and soon I was rolling along the backside of a breakwater looking west across Mahone Bay.

"Islands!" I blurted out. Yes, islands, but I had no idea which was which.

After reaching a loud *Private Property* sign at road's end, I turned back to what I took to be the best anchorage for a shoreside snooze. The spot I picked was marginal, strewn with boulders and bristling with sharp branches, but I managed to string up the hammock, arrange my sleep stuff and set up my kitchen on the rocks before the cloud-cloaked sun set. As the kettle boiled, I pulled on my red poncho and held my maps at arm's length to identify the islands. Little and Big Tancook were in line, so they looked like one big landmass, but I knew instinctively that the other, more distant one was East Ironbound Island. Rockbound, right there!

In an instant, as a slice of sun broke through and illuminated a tight stand of buildings on the island's north side, the whole novel shifted in my mind and became real. It had a lot to teach me about the way Joshua Slocum grew up, the world he lived and sailed in as a young man. By the time I dug into my bag-boiled chili, I'd transported myself there, across the water to David's new home, the tense and pungently fishy kingdom of Uriah.

Over the long groundswell of human history, ages come and ages go. Every historical age has a beginning and an end; the Age of Sail is no exception. From the mid-fifteenth to the mid-nineteenth century, global trade and military prowess relied on the billowing sheets of wooden sailing vessels helmed by men whose lives depended on full mastery of their craft. The Age of Sail had a good run, that's for sure.

And one age's demise is spurred by another's birth. The Age of Steam rendered quixotic the act of shipping cargo by sail, replacing the winds of chance with the surety of black-smoke propulsion. Within a generation, by the late nineteenth century, commercial sailing collapsed, and most clipper ships had their masts ripped off to become steamers and barges.

Joshua Slocum and David Jung—his fictional, spiritual cousin—were two of many thousands of career casualties, captains of ghost ships foundered on the shoals of history. Adapting to a fossil fuel–propelled future was the only option. David made the switch, but Slocum was an old dog resistant to anything that smacked of new tricks.

Slocum kept sailing when the world had given up on it.

Rockbound spirits a reader to the South Shore of Nova Scotia in the twilight of the Age of Sail, puts them on a sailboat alone and describes, in vivid sensory detail, what it takes to make that sailboat pay. David passes each successive test the author sets for him, rushing "quickly astern to fend her off the ledge" or "darting swiftly forward" to make the "halliards and creaking blocks sing." Then he's flying to "shove his tiller hard aport" and "darting forward" again to "hoist the jib and belay the halliard." His motions "swift and catlike," his bare feet "gripping the wet surface of thwart and washboard."

Even more than *Sailing Alone Around the World*, *Rockbound* evokes the vast store of knowledge and instinct Joshua Slocum had to have to stay afloat. For me, the fictional David Jung represented a direct conduit to Slocum's sailing soul.

By the end of *Rockbound*, every fisherman has an engine on his boat. When engines first appeared on the South Shore, they became must-have items. It was always a race to the fishing grounds and anyone with a sailboat was a last-place finisher, a laggard.

Slocum's desperate stunt was commercial sailing's last breath, its final nostalgic gasp. After Slocum, sailing went underground and resurfaced, in the early twentieth century, as a leisure pursuit, a passion project for the deep-pocketed.

A book like *Rockbound* is a fossilized record of a hard sailing life that, for better or worse, no longer exists.

I'm not quite sure how I slept that first night in the hammock, but I know it was post-sunrise when I ripped back the Velcro entry slit and dropped to the blue tarp I'd folded below.

I took my sweet time packing everything up. The whole "no schedule" world was settling on me, and I liked how it felt. Next to my barely hidden camp spot in the twisted bush was a freshly paved road itching to be skateboarded. I warmed up my legs with a rip on Chicken Tender. The slight downhill allowed me to lock into a close-footed surf stance, and I weaved in and out as if the yellow dashes were pylons.

The Ox stood tall as I hooked the last bungee and took a moment to admire him, his front wheel propped off the ground as if in anticipation of flight. Black and blue with a spot of red, that was my colour scheme by chance. It didn't occur to me until much later that these are the colours of bruises and scrapes respectively. That morning I was blinded by pride in my well-mannered road beast.

The Deck Restaurant in Blandford was more of a convenience store slash post office with an open kitchen in the centre and a few tables by the window overlooking Mahone Bay. Its domed wooden ceiling was covered by tea towels from around the world, each one with a unique story behind it. With miles to go before I reached Chester and—hopefully—the ferry to Big Tancook Island, I only had time to scarf the bacon and eggs Annie made me on the grill, which tasted heavenly, microwaved bacon notwithstanding. A quick and loud exchange with a nice local man sporting a hearing aid gave me some crucial intel: the weather—brisk but clear—and the ferry times.

Back on the road, one Aspotogan hill was enough to turn my mind to the task at hand, which was to finish the loop and backtrack to Hubbards to find the one address I'd scribbled in my notebook before leaving Cow Bay, the home of a certified psychic medium. Slocum had sought the same services in the wake of his wife Virginia's death at the unfair age of thirty-four. His grief at losing his soulmate and mother to their children gnawed at him continuously, so he found a spiritualist to conjure Virginia's ghost for one last conversation, hungry for a semblance of closure.

The results are lost to history, but Slocum, like the characters in *Rockbound*, put a good deal of stock in superstition and the tangible power of the spirit world.

My Conjuring Kit was ready, but after an arduous push through deep gravel, I learned the address was wrong, or maybe the psychic had a premonition and invented a false address to avoid an awkward Saturday morning conversation with an unannounced and obsessed surfer cyclist.

I took the hint and shelved my spiritual ambitions.

Soon the busy and rudely undulating Highway 3 to Chester gave rise to imaginary Peloton Guy, a red-faced and grinning man on a screen in front of me, barking out encouragement and telling me to "Dig deep" and "Go all in!"

When I stopped at the top of one hill to chug water, I saw a string of legitimate spandex-clad cyclists going the other way, their heads down and their rippling leg muscles pumping in unison. As much as I identified with them as cyclists, I knew where I stood: me and my labouring Ox, they and their purebred racehorses. Same road, different mode. Peloton Guy would always give me an E for effort, I knew that. No need to be envious.

I made the sailing mecca of Chester in a daze. Home of Chester Race Week, North America's largest annual keel boat regatta, this town tucked at the head of Mahone Bay had been the proving grounds of yacht folk since the mid-nineteenth century, when fishermen made a sport of racing each other—by sail power alone—to markets in Halifax and New England. Nowadays, Chester Race Week is a four-day party sponsored by Helly Hansen with the idyllic waters of Mahone Bay as racecourse. In Chester, I'd heard, you have to pay to play.

A *Lido Pool* sign caught my eye, and I followed it through the pretty residential streets to the waterfront, where I found a deserted crescent-shaped saltwater pool. The public washroom door was locked. Damnation! But I heard a voice say, "How's it going?" I looked down to the pool deck to see a young guy in red lifeguard gear and dark sunglasses.

"Hi," I called out. "Any reason this washroom's locked?"

He laughed. "Not sure, exactly. You can use the one down here if you need to."

"Excellent," I said, "and then...can I swim?"

Though the day was cool, and a breeze whistled off Back Harbour, the odd sun pop seemed enough to convince me a swim was a good idea.

"Ya, sure man," he said, "you'll be the first today!"

Matthew, the guard, did me a huge favour by letting me into the back-office washroom. I dumped my toiletry kit, my towel, and my change of clothes and emerged seconds later in swim trunks.

As I glided under water, I tried in vain to rub off the black grease streaks on my calves that were fast becoming my road tattoos. Matthew must have felt the need to look busy, because he grabbed the scoop net and started sweeping the clean surface for non-existent debris.

In the open wind, the only way to stay warm was to sit with just my head out of the water, so that's what I did, looking out over the long docks of Back Harbour, each one with its own large motorboat. Once out of the pool, I spent way too long in the lifeguard bathroom freshening up, which in my new vagabond world meant washing my face with actual soap, brushing my teeth meticulously, and applying generous swipes of deodorant.

"Thanks man," I said, when I walked out a brand new person. "Sorry about that."

"Ah, no probs," he said, "not much action around here today."

Feeling bold, and knowing I had to seize the opportunity, I asked Matthew if I could make a quick call home on the office phone.

"Sure, no worries," he said. The kid was a gem. I told him I'd be brief and dialled Genny's number.

The call buoyed me up even more. School was good, work was good, we missed each other lots, our deal to touch base every few days was intact. Any guilt I had for leaving evaporated.

Before I left to stash the Ox by the Tancook Ferry dock, Matthew and I shot the breeze for a bit. He was heading to Acadia University in a week after a whole year attending classes from a computer in his parents' basement, and I could see how excited he was to move out and meet actual humans his age. Our talk turned to surfing, and I asked if he might grant me one more favour: check the swell report for the upcoming week.

"Ok, it's loading," he said, "whoa, wow, that's crazy!"

"What?" I said, craning my neck to get a peek at the screen.

"Looks real big later in the week," he said.

"Hurricane Larry," I whispered, maybe too close to his ear.

I'd heard some rumblings about the storm brewing way down in the Caribbean, and Matthew's wave report confirmed what I hoped to hear. Larry was heading our way. I rubbed my hands together and narrowly avoided kicking up my heels right there on the Chester Lido Pool deck.

Matthew smiled. "You seem excited."

A note on surfers and hurricanes. As far as I know, surfers are the only subset of people who pray for hurricanes and bless them when they spin by. Boat owners? Hate hurricanes. Fishermen? Don't like them. Ferry operators, power grid workers, coastal homeowners? Loathe the 'canes. But to a surfer, this swirling dynamo is what we wait the whole year for, because the energy it pulses our way through the medium we love—seawater—morphs into big and powerful and scary waves. I'd chosen September for a host of reasons, chief among them to be out there for peak hurricane season. Larry was three days away, and I had to be ready.

Though I didn't look like a traditional pastel shorts and scarf-over-polo yachtsman, I at least felt somewhat spiffed up as I rolled slowly past the Chester Yacht Club, which I noticed had a bevy of high-end cars parked out front: shining Mercedes, BMWs, Teslas, and Audis. Nary a Toyota Yaris to be seen. A red Porsche convertible slipped past me as I pumped up a little side street of immaculately restored cedar shake houses, and I noted the telltale sign of the wealthy retiree: ball cap pulled low over a navy-blue high-collar windbreaker.

Chester had a scent, and that scent was money. A half-hour walk confirmed it. I knew I was being presumptuous and unfair, but I felt like Chester and I weren't meant to be, my feral quest at odds with its aristocratic air. After coughing up ten dollars for a pint of beer, I slunk back to the Ox, draped my wet gear on a park bench and pulled out my copy of *Rockbound* to spend my last hours before boarding the hour-long ferry to Big Tancook Island.

After I closed my book, I took a slow stroll to the end of an empty pier and enjoyed the view. Beneath puffs of cloud resting on a light blue sky, I could make out two green treeless islands — Meisners and Quaker — framing the dark aquamarine waters of Chester Basin. In the distance I saw one lone sailboat with its white sail flying, and my mind went to David Jung and Joshua Slocum, standing tall on their own decks, bathed in solitude and self-reliance.

I could see myself on my own sailboat out there, proud like them. Though a nagging voice reminded me that I knew next to zero about navigating one of those beauties, I could, at very least, stand there.

In a flash, I caught motion to my left, and there I saw a red sailboat gliding from the berths of Front Harbour toward me, her sails still wrapped snug.

"A real live sailboat," I said to a seagull holding down a pressure-treated piling next to me. "Maybe I'll get to watch it hoist the sails."

As it came closer, I made out a crew of four young men, none of them too anxious to "dart around" like David Jung. They all had beer cans in their hands, and they were passing a joint, huge plumes rising from each successive face. Over the outboard motor I could hear rap music. I realized that these guys were out for a pleasure cruise on one of their dad's boats. They probably wouldn't even hoist sails at all. As they passed by, one of them appeared at the stern, unzipped his fly with his beer-free hand, and took a long leak into the foamy wake. I cracked up. So this was Chester. I wondered what Josh would say about these jokers.

The clouded windows and persistent roar of the ferry made for perfect reading conditions, and I buried my head in *Rockbound* until I felt a harsh jerk. The dozen of us on board — some older ladies and a pair of disinterested teens — all stood up when we felt the slam of hydraulic ramp on concrete.

The Ox and I left last, and I immediately felt like I'd entered a different world. The pickup trucks leaving the wharf were dusty and beat-up, and none of them had licence plates. I watched their red tail lights crawl away up the gravel hill leading into the depths of dusky Big Tancook Island. With the sun fully set, a brief window of light remained to find a suitable camp spot and string up my hammock tent.

I powered up a rutted road and soon came face to face with three deer. "Hi," I said. They stared back at me. "Mind if I cut through?" More stares. I literally had to swerve around them. At a fork in the road I made a quick decision, and after rolling past three or four homes, one of which appeared to be a haunted junkyard, I came to a cobble beach facing the aptly named Southeast Cove. I was hoping to catch another glimpse of East Ironbound, but the darkness obscured my view.

I was surprised to see a bonfire on the beach with a bunch of people clumped around it, so I made a hasty call to cross a cratered parking area toward what I thought was a path into the stunted forest. I kept crouched as I came to a stop in a small clearing, worried the partygoers might turn hostile and drag me back to their inferno as a ritual sacrifice. Night thoughts, loud and clear, invaded my brain. But my decision was made for me by the darkness; I'd have to make the place work.

I strapped on my headlamp and turned it to the lowest setting, making sure not to face the beach. My hammock tent unfurled like a parachute, all canvas and tangled lines, and it took me minutes to straighten it out. Already I was coming to grips with the reality that my accommodation for the upcoming weeks on the road was a glorified Ziploc bag dependent on sturdy vertical objects set a specific distance apart.

"I'll make it work," I whispered to calm myself. "Everything's going to work out."

For hammock tent enthusiasts, the challenge is part of the appeal. With the right kind of forest, tenting in one of these can offer a unique sleep spot away from anyone with a traditional ground dwelling. I also reckoned a hammock tent would help me learn new knots, a kind of dryland training for my glorious sailing future. So I went all in.

Rigging up a hammock tent is a dance between tree selection and string pulling. Tie this, pull that, repeat. When done right, a taut fly roof sits jauntily above the hanging sleep compartment, a human-sized, banana-shaped cocoon. When done wrong, well…

It wasn't until I had my sleeping bag inside with headlamp and book in the handy mesh pocket that I realized one of my chosen trees was stone-dead. A closer headlamp inspection told me I'd be trusting my unconscious body to a piece of vertical driftwood.

"Really?" I hissed, hitting the dirt as two growling trucks raced by, sweeping my newest home with headlights. The wind had cropped up, and I could see the tree swaying like a metronome, back and forth.

The tent had to come down.

As the inky darkness thickened and the party noises notched up, I untied all the knots and carried the whole mess to my Plan B spot, which had better trees but way more jagged branches. Even though I worked fast, I could feel my hands cramping up in the cold. After a half-dozen jabs, one of which drew blood I couldn't see, I ripped open the tent's seam, placed my open sleeping bag inside, and took the plunge.

For hammock tenters, "the plunge" is the moment when you give yourself over to the tent, become one with it, trust it completely. When not erected in duress, this can be blissful. After a minute or so of struggling to get in your sleeping bag and finding the ideal angle for your body, the moment comes when you know you've found the sleep zone.

I was a shredded mess when I took my plunge on Big Tancook, and right away I knew it was wrong. Specifically, a large part of the surface area of my buns were on the ground. I stifled a laugh. *Perfect*, I thought, *all night dragging ass.*

After running through my options—none—I decided this would have to be my fate. My last worry, after twisting my earplugs into place to stifle the beach rager, was how I might make the morning ferry back to Chester—the only one all day—without an alarm clock.

Chapter 3

NIGHT MOVES

I talks wid myself, any man alone learns to do dat.
— *Rockbound*

What is it about the month of September that stirs the hearts of Nova Scotians? When asked, "What's your favourite month?" why is "September" on everyone's lips? And why does the mere mention of September cause a shivering, rubber-clad surfer in the flat slush of February to exhale a frosty sigh of yearning? It's simple. September is that magic span of days when the air is warm, the water is warm, the winds are calm, and—aside from the odd ripper of a hurricane—winter storms are a distant memory.

Yes, a Nova Scotian September is worshipped as a deity. The beaches, devoid of touristy hordes, seem to breathe freely again. Gorgeous, puff-ball cloud afternoons yield to psychedelic sunsets, and the shortening days only seem to make each slow-burn sunrise more accessible. Green continues to mean *go* for the deciduous trees, and it seems the leaves will never turn, especially on the South Shore, where monolithic oaks and elms and chestnuts form a grand canopy to sip cold drinks beneath.

And the ocean, the sweet Atlantic Ocean, our master and weather commander, well, let's just say September is the sea's most benevolent month. Its accrued warmth finally matches the temperatures of the land,

and the Fog Monster—who can easily frig up August, or *Fogust* as it's endearingly known—slips like a genie back into his bottle.

For teachers, September is complicated. When we show up for meetings in late August, we've finally attained peak flip-flop, a Zen state that only comes after our hyper-scheduled lives have completely dissolved. As we say, our wells have refilled, our batteries have recharged, we are ready, if not a tad reluctant, to resume our roles as energy-radiating ringleaders of positivity. Then we're handed our schedules.

This inevitable to-the-minute girdling of our existence makes the prospect of a clear and balmy September a bitter pill to swallow with our tepid staff-room coffee. I've sweated through many a dress shirt in afternoon classrooms full of exhausted, overheated teenagers, mopping my brow as I try in vain to drum up interest in the eight parts of speech or molecular bonding. On those glorious September days, the tranquil blue sky windowed above the heads of dozing adolescents feels more like an affront to the soul. And don't even tell me there's a groundswell running out there.

Hence the rare gift of a schedule-free September. I knew this was my one chance, my big moment to finally do September right. Before I left Cow Bay, I reasoned that abandoning all timepieces would harmonize me with the season, help me stay in trim with the glassy breaking wave that is the ninth and finest month. I could sip my freedom slowly and chase it with a shot of quenching solitude, schedules be damned.

Problem was, the Tancook ferry had a schedule, and since it was Sunday, the schedule showed only one crossing on that day of rest, and it would happen at 9:00 a.m. sharp.

When I woke up that morning in my sagging hammock tent, panic seemed to pulse from the sun. Judging by the quality of the light and the warmth of the morning, I figured it had to be dangerously close to 9:00. I'm not sure why it felt like a life-or-death ferry-make, considering I could have easily loafed the day away on sleepy Big Tancook, but I shot from my grounded cocoon like a New Yorker late for an important meeting.

I swore and sweated over each knot, balling the whole mess up and lashing it to the Ox in a frustrated huff. Instead of taking my time to bid farewell to East Ironbound Island, which sat five hundred metres away across a shimmering ocean expanse, I looked at it for three seconds before turning and pedalling like a madman across the washboard gravel.

Halfway back to the wharf, as I bumped past a pair of deer munching apples in a dew-smoke yard, the Tombstone came free and I shot my hand back to grab it, losing control of the handlebars. The deer barely flinched. At least I had a few witnesses to my gong show on wheels.

My heart sank when I saw the deserted wharf. I'd missed it. I'd overslept. Damn hammock tent. Now what? Why did I not bring a watch, a phone, a pet rooster? Fool move.

As I hung my sweaty head in defeat, I chanced a final look at the ferry terminal and did a double take. Either it was a mirage, or the ferry was still there, tied up since I'd rolled off twelve hours earlier. "Really?" I called out to no one. Yes really. A local in a rusty cube van confirmed that it was 8:00 a.m. I was an hour early.

I found a dusty corner of the wharf and scrambled up the concrete breakwall to look at the placid waters of island-studded Chester Basin. "Deep breaths, dude," I said, "deep breaths." With a much more measured pace, I extracted my kitchen box, fired up the stove until the water boiled, poured it into my camp French press and watched the grounds swirl and bubble. Nuts munched and dried mango chewed, I plunged the press and poured a steaming stream of dark brown goodness into my mug, snapping on the cap for good measure.

A few trucks bumped onto the wharf, and I watched the ferry workers emerge, walking so syrupy that I swore the world had gone slo-mo.

After some jumping jack flails to warm up, I returned to my coffee mug to receive the gift of the slow September gods. But wait. It looked, to my horror, like someone had dumped creamer on my mug. High above, a seagull the size of a mini fridge flew off, a satisfied flap to his wings.

"Crap!" I said, "bird crap!" Yes indeed, it was a blatant truth. The bird had dropped a chalky white mess on the very top of my coffee mug.

When it comes to loading up, the Tancook ferry does not mess around. I watched in awe as a hulking crane swung off the ferry deck, picked up a shed-sized metal box full of locals' gear, and plunked it down in the boat's stern. Being the only guy with a bike, I loaded up last and found a quiet spot up top, next to the flapping Nova Scotian flag.

As we left the concrete confines of the wharf, I looked back at Big Tancook Island with a tinge of regret. I'd rushed it. Ninety percent of my Big Tancook experience happened in the dark. The cheerful backlit houses crowding the cozy harbour seemed to be *tsk tsk*-ing me. *Isn't he supposed to be an explorer?* one little white house said. *Ya*, chimed in a yellow house with a pitched roof, *but he came flying in and out of here like a politician in election time!* The joke was squarely on me. I had to find a way, while still pedalling south, to slow down.

I ruminated on the debacle of a night I'd just endured. The darker side of September, I realized, was a literal shortening of days, an inexorable march to the equinox a few weeks away, a time when exactly half of any given twenty-four-hour day would be sunless. The previous September, I'd kept detailed notes on every day—weather, swell, wind, sunrise and sunset times—and I knew that our part of the Earth migrated away from the sun at a rate of four minutes a day; sunrise got two minutes later and sunset two minutes earlier. *Almost like a life*, I thought. A slow march into darkness.

Then this chestnut dropped: September's like my forties! Lots of brilliant days ahead, but summer's over, and all those hale and hearty leaves will have to flame out, dry up, and drop to the ground, only to skitter around for a few cold nights before being covered over, once and for all, with snow. I hadn't thought much about Night before I left, but the Tancook ferry ride drove home a truth: I had to embrace Night, I had to merge with the darkness. Somewhere in that pitchy veil were the vapour trails of Slocum's ghost.

Flying in the face of every guidebook ever, I skipped the UNESCO Heritage town of Lunenburg with the plan to absorb it from a distance and catch a sold-out, open-air concert I did not have tickets for. Tim

Baker, formerly of the great Newfoundland-born band Hey Rosetta!, was playing the new Lightship Brewery, and I'd scoped out a perch on some pilings I gambled would stay dry at high tide. I had my musical grifter's spot locked down but no idea where I'd sleep afterwards.

Between sound check and the show, I explored the vicinity and hatched a scheme to sleep in a field behind the Lunenburg golf course. It was part of a large lot topped by an obviously haunted and long-abandoned house, its boarded-up windows broadcasting neglect. Nothing about its dark mystery called to me, not at that stage of my voyage at least. The field had trees, yes, but they were giant oaks spaced well apart. Since the hammock tent and I were in a couple's squabble, I hatched a plan to try something new, something more...al fresco.

After drawing a diagram in my notebook, I snuck the Ox behind some bushes and quietly stripped him of his burden. From there I separated what I would need to realize my vision: both blue tarps, Therm-a-Rest, sleeping bag, and poncho-as-pillow. These I piled up and carried across the long grass to a stately tree. I laid one tarp down at its base and set about tying the other at a forty-five-degree angle off the oak, wrapping lines around its fat circumference as anchor and pegging the other end of the tarp where my feet would be. Tarps taut, I blew up my Therm-a-Rest and laid my sleeping bag over it, careful to fold the poncho into a thin but better-than-nothing pillow.

"This will work," I whispered, feeling like a mad scientist. "Yes, this will work...as long as it doesn't rain...but...this will work!"

From a distance the whole set-up exuded Cormac McCarthy's *The Road* vibes, but the sun was gone and the die was cast. Tim Baker would be on any minute and I'd have to hustle to get back to the harbour. My ad hoc hovel would have to do.

After a heavenly set of live music backed by the glimmering lights of Lunenburg, I returned to camp eager for sleep. The top tarp still held, but it was flapping in the breeze, a sound I would get to know intimately in the coming eight or so black hours. It was warm enough though, and a few mosquito bites confirmed it: I wouldn't freeze.

After a dry toothbrush with a squirt of water, I got into my bag fully dressed and stretched out. "Not too bad," I said.

The mattress, while slippery, kept the sharp stalks of dead grass from poking through. My final move was stuffing earplugs in and pulling my blue buff over my entire head to discourage the bugs. Exposed as I was, I felt somewhat secure, maybe even enough to fall asleep.

As my breathing deepened and my aching legs released their strain, a spotlight by the road turned on, bathing me in harsh white light. "Oh no," I said, popping right up. But it was just an automatic security light. I pulled the buff over my eyes and redoubled my commitment to stay. Aside from a barrage of tree droppings that pinged the tarp at odd intervals and a lone trumpeter swan offering up its tattered squawk to the night sky, I managed to get a rest that was obliquely related to a full night's sleep.

"Great white was seen in Green Bay recently, eh?" So said one of three retirees enjoying a Burger King breakfast on the sheltered patio next to the Irving gas station in Lunenburg. With a rainy Labour Day Monday ahead, they'd decided to bail on their golf plans. One gentleman in a PING hat liked my Tombstone, and he reckoned I needed to know just how many sharks were lurking in the exact waters I planned to surf when Hurricane Larry showed up.

That's it with non-surfers, sharks are a joke to them. But not for wave riders like myself, nor for sailors. Joshua Slocum was famously scared of sharks above all else. As he wrote, "For the admonition of sailors and sea bathers, generally, I say, put no faith in the yarn about harmless sharks." Fifty-foot seas thrilled him, but the spectre of being crunched by a great white sent him into visceral terror. No doubt his fear came from a seminal event in his seafaring past: once, in Cuba, he'd witnessed a shark bite a man in half.

"Watch out for fins!" the golfer called as I straddled the Ox in a steady rain. Very funny.

At that mid-morning moment, all I could think about was the wet road ahead and where I'd end up that night. I knew this Labour Day would be exceedingly laborious, dark storm clouds my only companions.

Still, I counted my blessings — the rain had waited until I'd secured everything in their waterproof shelters. Wherever I ended up that night, I'd be in a slightly damp sleeping bag instead of a sopping one. Perspective.

After a soggy, six-hour, white-knuckle ride, I pushed the Ox inland toward Voglers Cove and turned my thoughts to the upcoming sleep attempt, my fourth exposed night in a row. Deep South Shore wilderness surrounded me, and I knew I'd have to merge with it, a moist union if there ever was one.

Joshua Slocum had weathered many a rough night on the *Spray*, I rationalized, but at least he had a dry cabin to take shelter in. What did I have? A glorified Slip 'N Slide taco wrap.

"Maybe motel," I said. "Yes, motel. Dry sheets, towels, soap. Lying on a bed. Motel?" This was bad, I knew it. Motel thinking on an adventure is so soft, so gutless. I scolded myself for even entertaining it, pushing harder up the hills, but the thought, a kind of neon sign in my mind, kept flashing. *M O T E L.*

I knew from my map that the town of Liverpool was within striking distance; it was sure to have a motel. "No!" I yelled. "No motel. Not yet. Maybe in a few days, but not tonight. Tonight you find free shelter somehow."

This hilarious battle played out to an audience of no one. The road was devoid of cars. One glance into a quaint green bungalow with ornate white trim gave me the update: everyone was at home on their couch watching TV. If I caved and got a motel, I'd be joining the ranks, taking the e-bike easy road, giving up. I promised myself a future motel night, and set my sights on finding anything with a roof to hide under.

Once I'd resolved my dilemma, it happened fast. With a downhill head of steam, I made the split-second call to veer the Ox into some sort of community centre playground, nearly losing control as I came to a halt on a patch of tarmac littered with kid bikes, Tonka trucks, and Little Tikes cars. In the damp dusk, it appeared as though I'd stumbled on a hastily evacuated daycare. What really caught my eye was a steep-roofed board-and-batten storage shed with a sweet overhang, its one side out of view of a nearby house. It had two doors. I tried the first one — locked.

The second one, however, only had a gate latch. I creaked it open and there before me was a slice of road-weary cyclist heaven. A dark dusty cavity, maybe two by three metres, empty except for a push broom and one pink BMX bike with handlebar tassels. I jumped at the chance.

After a quick calculation that anyone in the neighbouring house would likely not see me, I went to work sweeping out the space, unloading the Ox, and lugging everything inside. I jury-rigged a way to keep the door closed by hooking a bungee cord into a knot in the wood and I stood there with my headlamp on, surveying my accommodations. I was in a pine coffin with vaulted ceilings.

"Home sweet home," I whispered.

The exposed studs were perfect shelves for my books and knick-knacks, so I laid them out to make the space homier. Next I tied my trusty brown rope—a remnant from an old Indiana Jones Halloween costume—across the space and hung up my soaked clothing. Finally, I laid out my sleep stuff on the folded tarp. Despite its crime scene ambience, I felt elation at avoiding another night in the hammock.

After dark, I ventured out for a quick survey of my surroundings. The strewn toys sat unmoved as I scanned each one with my headlamp beam. I crossed my fingers that I wouldn't freak out any small children in the morning, and as I walked past a basketball net with a shattered backboard, something white in the woods caught my eye. It was an arched sign laying on its side, partially covered in pine needles. I bent to read it and I felt the hair on the back of my neck stand up. *West Side Cemetery.*

Off to the right, in the bushes, stood a dozen or so untended tombstones. I was drawn in their direction, despite the feasting bugs. I knelt to illuminate one old slab and read what I saw.

In Memory of Ronald Freeman
Son of Herbert and Ella Conrad
Drowned August 18th, 1925
Aged 15 Years 13 Days

"God…" I gasped. A wave of sadness washed over me. The inscription below didn't bring any levity either. It was a piece of verse, laid out like a poem.

> *IN THE GRAVEYARD*
> *SOFTLY SLEEPING*
> *WHERE THE FLOWERS*
> *GENTLY WAVE*
> *LIES THE ONE WE LOVED*
> *SO DEARLY*
> *IN HIS LONELY SILENT*
> *GRAVE.*

The last line sent me scuttling back to the shed like a startled hermit crab. I bungeed the door, took a few deep breaths and crawled into bed to read *Rockbound* by headlamp. Hopefully the book could bring back those sweet sunny September feelings. Alas, the plot had thickened, and it was David's turn to face the merciless sea.

After establishing himself as a top fisherman on Rockbound, much to Uriah's deep chagrin, David jumps at the chance to join a fishing expedition to the Grand Banks. There his ship succumbs to an early season hurricane, foundering on the shoals of Sable Island. All hands are lost — except David, who is quick enough to lash himself to a piece of timber before he loses consciousness.

I closed the book. With my light off, the coffin feeling returned. *Drowning, what a way to go,* I thought.

When Joshua Slocum didn't return from his final voyage south, most assumed he had drowned. David, the fictional character, survived. Poor teenaged Ronald hadn't.

The sun I squinted into after squeaking open the lid of my pine box felt holy on my damp skin. A line from *Rockbound* crossed my mind like a stock ticker: "How he blessed the sun when it shone warm; the sun had been his best friend."

David loved the sun, and so did I. For the first time on my run to Brier Island, I saw that the sun offered wisdom. It made me feel safe. I knew I could handle a bunch of exposed nights if only the sun would pop out, hopefully with all that September promise, once in a while. I had one more day and night before Hurricane Larry was due, so I relished the assurance of what looked to be banner road conditions.

Tarp down on asphalt, I spread my junk out for maximum dryness and brewed coffee. As I walked around the deserted court, I saw a kid standing by the road waiting quietly for her bus.

"Right, school," I whispered.

As the still rural morning gave way to the squeal of air brakes and hydraulic doors, I savoured the quiet left behind. For fifteen years I'd always gotten on that bus; now, I watched it roll away. Yes, it was strange that I was squatting in some kind of post-apocalyptic daycare, but all of a sudden things felt right.

I soon found more unexpected wisdom as I urged the Ox through Voglers Cove, nearly crashing as I tried to appreciate the ancient oak and maple trees that seemed to grow inches from the road. A tidy, white century home with a single wooden chair out front caught my eye. Normally, I wouldn't stop to inspect someone's house, but this one was metres from the main road, and it had two hand-painted signs above a welcoming, wreath-clad door that said *A.J. Vogler* and *Home of Mac's Museum*. As I admired the Victorian architecture, a man in a blue-checkered jacket with an Eastlink ball cap came around the corner, pushing a red wheelbarrow.

"Hi there," I said.

"Hello," he replied, easing down on the sole chair. He had clear blue eyes, bushy white eyebrows, and a wide smile.

"Is this your museum?" I asked.

"Yessir," he said. "Wanna have a look?"

"Really?" I blurted out. I'd taken it to be closed, maybe for good. "Oh, yes please."

"Go on in," he said. "Have a look around. I'm just gonna finish cuttin' the grass. I'll check with ya in a few."

I knew I was in heaven as soon as I crossed the threshold. On either side of the frayed carpet runner were glass display cases backed by walls of wooden shelving, every surface crammed with interesting stuff. Old board games, clocks, antique shoes, butter crocks, painted teapots, creepy Halloween masks—it was like someone's imagination had exploded. Under the glass was a fascinating world of ephemera. Ancient broaches, gleaming watches, yellowed stamp collections, little leather-bound books. I stood there slack-jawed, my eyes darting from one neat thing to the next. After what could have been five minutes or fifty, I heard the bell jingle and the front door open.

"Whaddya think?" a hoarse voice called out.

"Wow," I stammered, "this museum is...it's so...interesting."

"Thanks, young fella. Everything's for sale by the way."

"No way."

"Yessir. Slowly shuttin' her down. I'm eighty-five, so I've already lived about ten years more than I thought. Time to find homes for all this stuff, eh? Can't take it with me."

He chuckled and tipped his hat back on his forehead. I hadn't noticed his wrinkled hands before, but now I knew for sure that I was in the presence of a man advanced in age. As he leaned on the glass counter, I gave in to my curiosity and peppered him with questions. He was keen to oblige.

His name was Mac Morse, and he'd run Mac's Museum for forty years. His father-in-law, A.J. Vogler, had run it as the village general store for a few generations before that. In its heyday, it was a post office, a dry goods store, an apothecary, and a fabric shop.

"He sold everything," Mac said. Whatever the community needed, A.J. Vogler brought in.

Mac told me A.J. was five foot three but strong as five men, a real character with a storehouse of tales from the wild rum-running past. The building we stood in had actually been across the road, much closer to the water, but A.J. had moved it across single-handedly, using only a team of oxen to do the job. When he died in 1983, the whole town came to see him off.

"I'm almost there myself," Mac said.

I wasn't sure how to respond. Was he talking about his own death? Why was he smiling?

"Yep, I'm old and decrepit. That's why I still mow the lawn — gotta keep moving. Not sure if I'll be here next year."

I knew this wasn't morbid humour. This was wisdom. Mac knew where he was heading, and he seemed almost happy about it. I could tell by his sunny countenance that he had no regrets about his life up to that very moment.

"Nice thing," he said, "is that my daughter and her husband moved here from the city. Helps them save money, and they get an old fella like me to take care of. Decent trade I'd say."

We laughed. Mac was, at his core, just a nice guy. I took note.

Before I pedalled on, I had to acquire some fresh ingredients to add to my Conjuring Kit. Mac gave me a few minutes to pick my treasures. When he came back, I had them lined up on the glass countertop.

"Are you sure these are for sale, Mac?" I asked. It felt like a violation to buy museum exhibits.

"Oh yes, yes," he chuckled, "as they say, everything must go."

I had exactly five items in mind: a tiny magnetic pin in the shape of a ghost, a slim leather-bound copy of *The Vampire* by Rudyard Kipling, a pocket-sized book of Temperance Chimes — sheet music with song titles like "Oh! Touch Not the Wine Cup," "Beautiful Water," and "Father's a Drunkard and Mother's Dead," published in 1873 — a licence plate with a *Hee Haw*-looking horse braying out *I Love Country Music*, and, my impulse buy, a brittle pirate mask with elastic bands still in place.

Sheepishly, I looked at Mac and asked him how much.

He paused and scanned the goods. I noted the deep grooves in his face.

"How's ten bucks sound?" he said.

I was ready to pay at least thirty for the lot. "Deal!"

After he signed the Tombstone with my silver Sharpie, I stashed my treasure and readied myself for the road. We both looked toward the sun. I thanked him again.

"Thank you for your business," he said, "and safe travels now."

My last thought as I set off was to never forget Mac's lesson. Kindness, openness, generosity, gratitude for a life well lived. Now it was my turn to smile.

As sweet as that warm September breeze was, my body was crying out for rest by the time I took a dead-end gravel road into East Berlin in search of a place to camp. My knees broadcasted pain signals; knees weren't meant to be perpetual motion pistons, at least not my forty-four-year-old ones. I knew I had to pick my dead ends wisely. Every downhill would bite me on the way back up.

The approaching swell was on my mind too. I had to rest up for Larry. Counting back three nights, it was (1) pseudo sleep in a failed hammock, (2) damp oak tree tarp, and (3) rock-hard barnboard. I needed a dialled-in, comfortable hammock spot to truly find the superior rest my friends raved about. That's why, as the gravel road swung down to a surprise sandy beach, I decided to go public with my sleep intentions.

On a low cliff overlooking a long cobble hook, I found a stand of sturdy pines that had been limbed to open the sunrise view. Even better, the land around was innocuous soft grass sprinkled with buttercups. It looked like Bambi's birthplace. To camp here would be blatant trespassing. There was a trailer about fifteen metres away. It looked uninhabited though, which meant this dreamy little grove overlooking the ocean was primed and ready for an intrepid surf cyclist like myself. The two cottages across the road didn't bother me—if someone came by, I'd ask permission or at least plead my case for local mercy.

I quickly and quietly strung the hammock up between two perfectly spaced trees, pegged it out tight, adjusted the fly, and organized my other gear in a little village beside the Ox. Still no one came around, so I took my snacks and walked barefoot down the secluded beach, where I came across a wonderland of geological beauty.

Smooth granite ridges held hidden tidal pools at every turn, and I stood mesmerized by the bright yellow underwater kelp drifting lazily in and out with the swell. For a few minutes, I forgot who and where I was. South Shore beauty in September sun can have that effect.

Of course, my stomach rumbled me out of that reverie, and I fed it an Eat-More bar and some fresh beef jerky, hoping to keep the stove stowed for a potential hasty exit. Just as I finished chewing and admiring the pinky-purple glow on the horizon, my plot for the night thickened in a most unusual and terrifying way.

By narrowing my eyes, I made out a man in a pink shirt circling my camp, poking around in my gear.

"Go time," I said, hustling back in his direction.

But just before I climbed the rocky rim, something caught my eye about a hundred metres away down the cobbles. At first I thought it was a black dog, but there were no people nearby. Strange for a dog to be out there alone…and it was a big dog, really big. Then the dark blob stood up on its hind legs and sauntered deeper into the low-tide seaweed. It was no dog. It was a real-life, right-over-there black bear.

I jumped up the rocks as if I'd stepped on a mousetrap. Mr. Pink Shirt was gone. I scrambled up to my hammock and looked at the bear, hoping it was just a figment of my imagination. Not so much. There he was, foraging around the rocks, far enough away that I wasn't worried for my immediate safety, but close enough to make spending a night in a thin canvas bag inadvisable.

As my mind blanked and my quick decision skills evaporated, an actual dog started barking in my direction. There was Mr. Pink Shirt eyeing me from back up the road. What to do? Involuntary muscles took me toward him, barefoot on gravel. When I got close, I spilled my guts.

"Hello! I'm Ryan. I'm biking and surfing down the South Shore, looking for Joshua Slocum. That's my hammock tent. I'm hoping to stay the night. Well, I *was* hoping—is this your land?"

The dog kept hacking, but Mr. Pink Shirt said nothing. After an excruciating pause, he smiled.

"It's not my land," he said. I caught a whiff of an English accent. "But I'm sure the owner would be fine with you camping over...how long do you plan to stay?"

"Oh, I'll be gone first thing," I said, "you won't even know I was here."

"Sounds fine to me then," he said.

"Oh, great," I said, oddly not relieved, "but wait, I'm pretty sure I saw—actually, I can see it now—ya, there's a bear right down the headland."

He grinned even wider. Was that a sinister grin? "A bear? Right, yes, well, he's a friendly bear."

"A...friendly bear?"

"Friendly chap, he is. You've nothing to worry about."

And that's how he terminated the conversation. Seriously. I stood there gingerly, feeling the sharp rocks. A bear. A black bear. A friendly black bear. I looked at my picturesque camp spot suffused with a now deep-purple sky. It looked so cozy. Maybe that bear was far enough away. He didn't look like a "problem bear," right? I mean, he's over there eating snails or something. He'll be stuffed pretty soon. Won't even come close. Chances are he'll just amble back into the woods. Right?

Joshua Slocum was the master of catching forty winks in dangerous places. How many times had he reefed sails and slipped into the *Spray*'s cabin as the sea ran roughshod around him? He could override a tempestuous psyche. There's an art to sleeping with the enemy at the door.

It took every ounce of fear-squashing to rip the Velcro open and roll into the hammock. There, immense vulnerability lurked.

I tried to think of surfing, of a clean, endless wave breaking down a cobblestone point. To no avail. The beast was in my head, toying with my bravery.

"I'm a bear buffet in a bag," I whispered, shuddering with silent laughter.

LARRY'S GHOST

Haunts or no haunts, I stays. I ain't skeered o' no haunts.
— *Rockbound*

A thin mist slipped under the sun as I paddled my Tombstone into deep water, pulling for a spot to collect my thoughts and study this new-to-me wave. With no one else out, I did my best to calculate how fast the wave was moving, where the takeoff spot was, what kind of big wave set frequency I was dealing with, and, most crucially, what awaited me under water if I crashed on the drop. With practice, an eyeball survey like this can happen almost instantaneously, but it's always helpful to watch a local take a wave before joining a line-up. Come to think of it, why wasn't anyone else on it?

The head-high wall seemed to materialize from nothing. A ghost wave. I noted where it stood up on its haunches and opened a steep face before rocketing foam down the line, and I decided I would avoid that spot at all cost. No pitching lip heroics for me. Who would drag my lifeless body up the rocks if I smashed the bottom? No, I would play it safe and hang halfway down the shoulder to catch the freight train where it wasn't so juiced.

The wave, I knew, was what we surfers call a "slab." Slab waves come fast through deep water, hit a reef or rock ledge at full speed, and rear up, sucking water from the shallows before detonating shut in a violent clampdown. A surfer simply has to slide through the tube before being crushed, easy as that. The most famous slab wave in the world is Teahupoo (pronounced *Cho-poo*) in Tahiti, a wave so big and beautifully destructive that only the most unhinged attempt it.

By calling the wave I was eyeing a slab, I knew I was drifting into hyperbole-town. In Nova Scotia, we use the word "slab" to describe a steep wave breaking over a sudden shallow object—usually a granite ledge—but our slabs are toddlers compared to the fully realized adult slabs of the Pacific Northwest, Scotland, Tasmania, and fabled Tahiti. Still, with the right swell conditions, our junior slabs can produce hollow, overhead waves that will twig-snap your board if you go over the falls.

I'd had slabs in mind when I asked my friend Tony to shape a board for my South Shore journey, but I was pondering a different kind of slab. Gravestones, those dark markers of departed souls, have the same nickname. Cemeteries are full of vertical slabs, and standard gallows humour might describe a recently deceased body as "lying on a slab." If I had a surfboard that looked like a tombstone, I fantasized, maybe it would give me exclusive access to Slocum's realm.

In a fit of land-based inspiration, I'd even asked Tony to put "Here Lies RC Shaw" in old-timey graveyard font beneath a winged skull right on the top deck of my board, sprayed a sinister dark grey. I felt pretty clever back then, but there was zero humour as I straddled it and watched the ocean heave in front of me. What kind of fool messes with death that way? Not cool. I hitched forward and buried the nose to obscure the lettering.

One last image flashed up before I mustered the courage to approach the peak. It was Bob Simmons, the eccentric math whiz and inventor of the modern surfboard, paddling out in dangerous conditions at Windansea Beach in Southern California, circa 1954. Prior to that fatal session, Bob had revolutionized wave riding by bringing hydrodynamic theory to surfing. Before Simmons, surfboards were unwieldy wooden logs. The advent of hollow core balsa shapes lightened boards considerably, but their lumpish outlines limited speed and control. Simmons was a speed lover above all else. He knew that planing hulls, used with success in World War Two beach-landing crafts, held the key, so he set about building boards with parallel lines and wide tails, placing two keel fins in the back corners to reduce drag. His creations were fast, loose, and skate-y, so fluid that a surfer had to learn how to check speed to stay in the pocket of a breaking wave.

The seeds of the shortboard revolution of the late 1960s were planted by Bob Simmons. No one had brought a mad scientist's approach to surfboard design before, and the results were undeniable. Tragically, he wasn't around to see it grow. He drowned that day at Windansea, only thirty-five years old. A witness said he fell on a huge wave, his board arcing up like a breaching whale to land on his head, knocking him unconscious. His body washed ashore a few days later. Simmons was on my mind because my board, my Tombstone, was a planing hull just like Bob's, a shape that's now known around the surf world as a "mini Simmons."

"Stop thinking and go!" I heard myself say.

Pep talks are necessary when surfing alone. I wished a buddy was out there to hoot me into my chosen wave, but no dice. There it was, peeling toward me, a clean shoulder-high blue wall, its bladed crest tempting me to join the energy party.

A few deep strokes and I felt the Tombstone pitch forward, a lurch I used to pop to my feet and angle down the line. All thoughts evaporated as I whipped across the foggy face, crouched into a backside rail grab stance known as "pig dogging," an unglamorous but effective way to hold the highest speed possible. This was flight, I was flying. I broke into a grin just before I made out a curve in the wave that meant only one thing—no graceful exit for me. As the lip folded over, I ejected and locked my arms into roll-cage position to protect my head from whatever came next. It was a merciful tumble. I let my body find its way to the surface of the foamy, pungent brine, then yanked my leash to recover the Tombstone. A quick scramble up the greasy rocks and I was out of the water, safely on dry land once more. I offered up a mental high-five to Bob and Tony for their part in my one-wave session and made for the boulders, where I sat and watched wave after wave haunt the bright grey shroud of a sun-blotted sky.

Lunch at the Liverpool Legion was a gift from Neptune himself. After a sunny post-surf road slog, the sandwich board proclaiming "fish chowder special" put the Ox and I into full skid mode. When I walked in, the handful of patrons and kitchen staff stopped in their tracks and stared my way. They weren't smiling.

I knew I looked weary and scorched, but was it something else about me that offended their sensibilities?

Just as I risked a sniff of my armpits, a gruff woman behind the canteen-style kitchen window said, "Your hat, dear."

"Oh!" I stammered, "right, sorry about that."

Here I was trying for an incognito entrance, and I'd broken the cardinal Legion rule. At their core, Royal Canadian Legions are bastions of respect for our military forebears, our veterans. All that me-time had me forgetting my manners. The locals tuned me in.

After ordering the fish chowder and an egg salad sandwich, I took my big glass of water and sat at the only seat left, joining five locals at their long table. My chair squeaked as I sat down.

"Hello gentlemen," I said, "hope you don't mind if I join you."

"Gentleman?" one guy with a thin moustache and a missing tooth joked. "Best thing I been called all day. Of course, saddle up."

The b'ys seemed part of a loose collective of regulars, and I could see by the strewn three-dollar drafts that this was happy hour. I scanned the room to confirm—between the glass case stuffed with military antiques and the VLT machines, the clock told me it was 2:00 p.m. I tucked into my food with gusto and listened to the conversation flow.

"First drink with this hand all day," Mr. Moustache joked, lifting his glass with his left.

Before he could finish, a man with slicked-back hair and chunky hearing aids chimed in with, "Already had two with his other hand."

"Gotta exercise the whole body, right?" Mr. Moustache fired back.

From there, talk turned to the Blue Jays' playoff run—"Ain't makin' it"—to the federal election—"No majority, can't see the Tories gettin' in"—to Hurricane Larry. That's where I lit up and found the courage to join the banter.

A third man, clean-shaven with a Jays hat cocked high on his head, spun us a yarn about some crazed cocaine smuggler who'd just stolen a sailboat in Halifax Harbour and sailed it down to the Caribbean. The day before, the boat's owner got a random call from the US Coast Guard, telling him his personal locator beacon had pinged from the eye of Hurricane Larry. The owner whipped down to the Armdale Yacht Club and, sure enough, his boat was gone.

"Not too smart, that fella," said the clean-shaven man in a New England-ish twang I'd never heard before. "Clears Halifax only to sail into the teeth of a hurricane. Musta been in big trouble if he set off that beacon, eh?"

This was how I gleaned intel on predicted surf conditions. In pre-internet days, the "coconut wireless" was essential for surfers to make strike mission decisions. As much as I hoped the desperate boat thief hadn't been lost at sea, my selfish surf brain started daydreaming about the waves awaiting me down the road beyond Liverpool.

Tempted as I was by a draft beer-soaked story session with the Legion locs, I knew I had to pull the chute. Mr. Moustache hit me with some words of wisdom as I stood up to leave.

"You gotta live today," he said, chuckling, "cuz there might not be a tomorrow!"

With that nugget stowed in my cortex, I ground the Ox's gears and laboured up the sweeping, aptly named Hospital Hill away from Liverpool's Main Street. My map told me this route—Shore Road—was a loop, so I'd be back in Liverpool no matter what, hopefully after a hero's dose of that most coveted Scotian surfer staple: hurricane swell.

What do Beth, Noel, Ginny, Dorian, and Juan have in common? If you said they're a mariachi band, you're likely not from Nova Scotia. That slew of names, along with many others, represents destructive storms that have slammed the province over the years. Looking at their tracks from Africa through the Caribbean all the way up the gut of the Atlantic tells you that our fair province juts squarely out into Hurricane Alley.

Hurricanes are no joke around here, especially after 2003's infamous Hurricane Juan spun into town with Category 2 force. Carrying winds of 160 km/h, Juan made landfall just outside Halifax and left a path of destruction that cost $300 million in damage and, tragically, took eight lives. It was the worst storm to hit the city since 1893. Folks had no collective memory of a direct hit that bad, so most were underprepared. After the power was restored a week later and many of the uprooted trees were removed from garage roofs, there was a run on generators. My beloved *Silva* was just one of many boats to bust her moorings and wreak havoc on the waterfront.

Every June I look for the inevitable "Blow by Blow Predictions" newspaper headline for the upcoming hurricane season, which runs from late June until early November. When a storm starts brewing down south, news articles appear, reminding us that "it would be a good idea to secure the lawn furniture and put away the barbeque," and as it gets closer, more pinpoint headlines like "Hurricane Teddy could hit NS by Tuesday" encroach on page one. We jump online to check out the latest track predictions, which always look like some kind of north-reaching snow cone. It's the unpredictability that captures the imagination. "Oh, it's tracking for landfall closer to Boston," we say, or, "Looks like it will hook off for Europe," or, "Yikes, we're right smack in the middle of the cone." It could be days away, the sun shining and the breezes mellow, and we have no idea what might happen—shredding destructo wind, big rains, or absolutely nothing. Sailors beware, surfers prepare.

When a hurricane tracks our way, I can't help but share my enthusiasm with unsuspecting students. Science class takes a quick detour to the anatomy of hurricanes. "A hurricane is a kind of tropical cyclone," I rant. "The ocean has to be at least 26.5 degrees Celsius—hot, eh? Winds off Africa rip over the warm water so the moist air rises fast. As it jets up, what has to happen?" Silence. "Anyone?"

A hand pops up.

"The warm air cools," some keener says.

"Yes!" I praise, "you know your thermodynamics. Yes, it cools and condenses into giant storm clouds. That cooling moisture releases a ton of heat."

Half the class is locked in now, if only to see where their nutty surfer/teacher's energy will go next.

"Convection, right?" I say. "What does a convection current create?"

"Wind!" blurts another student.

"Yes! Exactly. Strong winds. All that fast-moving air creates an area of low pressure, which becomes the centre of the hurricane, or the…"

"Eye!"

"Right, right, the eye. Once the eye forms, it's on. The storm gets hungry for warm water, and if it finds it, it grows. By the time it joins the Gulf Stream, that ocean current running south to north, it's given a human name, like…"

"Juan! Hey, how come the names are human names? Who decides? Like, why not just make up funny names, like, I dunno, Gorgonzo or something?"

Here's where every teacher hits a crossroads. Take the bait and go on a walkabout that might lead to an education-less abyss or get back on track.

"We'll come back to that, I promise," I might say. "But the hurricane is big now, you can see its white clockwise swirl on the radar. Now it's all about track. Where will it make landfall? This largely depends on the weather systems inland. Up here in Nova Scotia, we are lucky enough to watch from a distance. But once in a while a hurricane swirling down there for days will take off like a shot and run straight for us. If our waters are warm and there's no high-pressure system to protect us, it's collision time."

The awkward silence is a perfect segue to our lesson on mitosis. Just as I'm about to turn back to the board, I catch a hand up.

"Yes, question."

"Hey Mr. S, aren't you a surfer? Like, how do hurricanes and surfing relate?"

It's a trap, I know. After years in the classroom, it's blatantly obvious when a student attempts to lure a teacher off the task at hand. Unfortunately, this subject is my Achilles heel. Of course I bite.

"Great question," I say, catalyzed, "as far as I know, surfers are the only humans who actually like hurricanes and who actively pray for their arrival. Here's why…"

Knowing smiles tell me the students have bagged their prey.

"Ocean storms create waves, right?" Heads nod. "Wind energy transfers to the surface of the water and creates wave energy. Wave energy radiates out in all directions, just like when you drop a pebble in a pond. Hurricanes are the ultimate energy monsters, so they create maximum wave energy wherever they go. The bigger the radius of the hurricane, the longer that energy will pulse. But surfers need hurricanes to follow an ideal path for the waves to be clean and surfable. Juan's path, for example, was no good for surfing—it made landfall right near where we're sitting today. The ocean was too chaotic, too disorganized. Same with Dorian. In fact, Dorian swept over Cow Bay—the winds were crazy—and I remember coming outside in an eerie quiet and realizing we were smack in the storm's eye. I ran back in when the wind started howling again from the opposite direction. What we want is for a hurricane to move north through the Atlantic, slowly, and hook away from us toward Great Britain. If that happens, the wave energy travels farther and organizes into bigger, cleaner sets of waves, which break when they hit land. The added bonus is the offshore wind the hurricane draws with it. Offshores clean up a wave's face and create the perfect canvas for surfers to paint."

"So shouldn't you be surfing right now?" I hear from the same student.

"Haha, I wish…now back to mitosis, eh?"

At that moment the bell always rings, and I'm left scrambling as my crew packs up and shuffles past me. Ah, teaching.

The sun held and blessed the rest of the day, bleeding into an other-worldly sunset that illuminated a thick layer of billowy clouds. By the time it was dark, I'd scoped out some promising wave set-ups, paddled out in pounding beach break, and eaten a steaming bag of chewy beef stew. The day's waves were forerunners from Larry, I knew, so the next day would be bigger and more powerful.

All around me the air was suffused with ocean spray, the roaring drone muting any birdsong I might have heard. When I wriggled into my hammock and found a semi-comfortable sleep posture, I stuffed my earplugs as deep as I could to dampen the sound. It was just like being on an airplane.

The next day arrived wet, so I packed up in the drizzle and made for the spot—a right point break—I knew would be working. After gorging on gorp and strong coffee, I pulled on my wetsuit, waxed my Tombstone, and headed for the line-up, which consisted of one guy wearing a helmet. The waves were large and loud, and I could barely get through the gnashing whitewash. A touch of doubt crept in as I paddled toward the other guy, a local I hoped. I watched a couple of waves push through, and then I yelled out, "Pretty big, eh?"

"Real big!" he called back. Typical surfer small talk.

"Hey," I said, "I'm curious. How come you're wearing a helmet?"

Just then a face opened up and before he could answer he was gone. I watched as he disappeared, only to come flying out in a wall of spume way down the cove. When he got back to where I was apprehensively floating, he said, "Helmet's for that," and nodded at the wave's drop zone.

I made out a curious swirl of water on the otherwise clean surface. It was a stove-sized boulder covered in seaweed.

"At mid to low tide you gotta watch out for that," he barked.

"Damn," I said. A collision with that bad boy might be a session-ender.

Somehow the local always missed it though, zipping to his feet and finding the high line as the wave broke clean behind him.

After some fun rides down the wave's shoulder, I decided to flirt with the boulder a bit, its boil-ish presence pulling me closer and closer. I'd watch the horizon for the next set, pick what I thought was a good takeoff, and find—just as I started paddling—that it was always *right there* in my line.

Two aborted drops later I decided to commit. Helmet Man hooted at me to indicate a choice wave and I swung the Tombstone and started digging, paddling with all my might to gain speed for the pop up. At the critical moment when I had to stand, my board chattered and my hands slipped, bringing my knee down hard on the top deck.

The wave rag-dolled me and I was gone in a vortex of angry foam, lost, at the mercy of the Surf Gods, who promptly raked me over the boil in an oddly gentle way. I kissed the boulder really. When I finally shot to the surface like some confused cork, I knew my session was over. I hauled the Tombstone up under my arm and scrambled over the rocks before the next wave sluiced past, pausing only once to look back as the local was doing his best Super Dave Osborne impression on an overhead bomb.

"You all right?" I heard from the road. A few more surf mobiles had pulled up to check the conditions. I made out a Willie Nelson look-alike pulling on his wetsuit behind a Sprinter van with out-of-town plates.

"Ya, I'm good," I responded. "My board, not so much."

I held it up for inspection and there it was: a baseball-sized impact crater just off the centre, right in the Tombstone's heart.

"Nasty ding, man," he said. "I'm Buster, by the way. You're not from around here, are ya?"

I spun out my yarn about biking down the coast in search of Slocum and surf, and he told me his. The plates said South Carolina, but he had a little place nearby. His wife was in the van looking at photos she'd taken of the waves. Though Buster and his lady had southern twang accents, I could tell they'd put in their time and become South Shore locals themselves. Buster noted what I'd been hearing lately, especially back in Cow Bay: the waves were getting more crowded now that everyone was travelling again.

"Even still," he said with a smile, "beats the craziness back home in the US."

Buster was seventy-three and still paddling out in big waves, though he'd mellowed out a bunch. As he talked about the crowds at the South Carolina beaches, he dropped some honesty on me.

"I used to be the biggest asshole in the water," he said, "then I grew up."

Nowadays, he was thankful to even be surfing at all. Just the year before he'd had a heart attack in the waves. If his buddies weren't there to pull him in, he'd be dead for sure. And he wasn't the only one—two friends even younger than him had given up the ghost while surfing, both from heart attacks.

"Heavy," I said.

But Buster was still standing. In fact, he was waxing up his mid-length and preparing to get out there. Before we parted ways, he gave me the surf report. Rain overnight, clearing midday, wind north and squarely offshore, Larry's swell maxing out by late afternoon.

"Thanks, Buster," I said.

"Any time," he called back over his shoulder, grey hair flying. "And fix that board up tonight!"

I considered staying in my wetsuit for the rainy ride back to Liverpool but declined; I didn't need any more help to look like a road clown.

As I felt my legs burn and thought of my injured Tombstone, my wet hammock tent, and my damp everything else, I resolved to get soft and cave on a motel room. Visions of a hot shower, sleeping with an actual pillow, and maybe, just maybe, indulging in a pint or two of cold beer coursed through me, and I found a last reserve of energy to push back down Liverpool's oak-lined Main Street, across the Mersey River bridge, and up to the doors of Lane's Privateer Inn.

I asked for the cheapest room and that's what I got, though to me it was like Versailles. Creaky, worn, dated, clean, perfect. Within an hour, it looked like something had exploded in there, my gear strewn on every surface, my panniers hung up, knick-knacks on every ledge. When I sunk, utterly exhausted, into the tub of scalding water, I entered an odd state of consciousness that seemed equal parts sleep, wakefulness, and death.

After what felt like a compression of eons later, I emerged a new and insatiably hungry human. I mashed the last of my dried mango in my mouth and set about fixing the Tombstone for peak Larry.

Ding repair on the road is the embodiment of a Band-Aid solution: I stripped back the wax with the aid of a hair dryer and scraper, sanded the impact crater to ready it for sealant, and squeezed way too much sun cure resin into the hole. A surfer must prevent water from infiltrating the foam core. Sun cure is a crude and ingenious solution, but it relies on actual sunshine to harden the resin. If it's cloudy, as gunmetal grey Liverpool was, the gash stays moist. I slathered the sun cure on and crossed my fingers that the next day would sun up.

A spooky, mind-bending thing would happen to me in Lane's Privateer Inn around the midnight hour, but the time between was dedicated to consumption. I was hungry for real food, connection with home, Liverpool lore, and, oh hell yes, Hell Bay beer, specifically what I considered the Liverpudlian brewery's finest concoction, its peerless English Ale.

In the snug, recently renovated pub downstairs, I ordered a pint and a haddock burger. To fill the time as my salivary glands went berserk, I did what any amateur historian would do. I read the back of the menu.

Liverpool's nickname is Port of the Privateers for good reason. Like most port towns on the Nova Scotian coast, it went from ancient seasonal camp of the Mi'kmaq to New France trading harbour to New England Planters settlement, flip-flopping from an American sympathizer during its 1776 Revolutionary War to a staunch defender of the British Crown in the War of 1812.

The place I was sitting patiently in, dabbing my mouth and trying to ignore the volcanic sounds of my stomach, was likely the main parlour of a grand house built in 1798 by Joseph Barss Sr., a politician and sea captain. With three storeys, four rooms per floor, and a fireplace in every room, the Barss home was one of the largest in Liverpool. The town had a good run in the nineteenth century, dominating the timber trade and holding down a top spot on the shipbuilding ladder.

Joseph Barss Jr. took his sea captain's inheritance to the next level, becoming Liverpool's most successful and famous privateer. As captain of the *Liverpool Packet*—a schooner bristling with cannon—he captured at least fifty American vessels in the run-up to the War of 1812.

As I found out at the Queens County Museum, it's a grievous error to mix up *privateer* and *pirate*. Pirates raided for themselves, but privateers pillaged for the Crown, carrying a physical letter of marque from whoever's figurine was atop the royal cake. When I attempted to sum up a privateer as a "pirate with a hall pass" the museum curator threatened to hang me from the gibbet.

Like most privateers, Barss Jr.'s luck finally ran out when, in 1813, he lost a hard-fought battle with a superior American vessel. After several months of harsh imprisonment, he was set free on one condition: never to sail again. He took the deal and left for the Annapolis Valley, leaving his stately home to become, eventually, an inn for wayward dirtbag surf cyclists.

O, the haddock burger! O, the ale! My neurons blazed new pathways of ecstasy, and I had no choice but to brave the downpour in search of more delight. At an exposed pay phone, I stood in the deluge and poured my heart out to Genny and the girls. When I walked off, full of love and a detailed swell forecast, I felt like Gene Kelly in *Singin' in the Rain*.

I made a jaunty beeline for the Hell Bay Brewery, where the only other patron to dare the tempest was an actual Englishman around my age. He'd recently pulled up stakes in Alberta's oil patch and bought a fixer-upper house in Liverpool with cash, so he had the skinny on the local nightlife, which consisted of a speakeasy attached to an old bowling alley.

Of course I followed him there when Hell Bay closed, and he wasn't lying. It was an immaculate and utterly empty candlestick bowling alley, just waiting for the silence to be broken by a thundering strike, which happened a half-hour later, when the Englishman and I parted ways, and I joined an eclectic Halifax-based painting crew for a no-holds-barred bowling extravaganza. Once the paint crew left, I returned my clownish size-twelve bowling shoes and entered the night alone, ready to poke around sleeping Liverpool in search of the spiritual.

I had to tour the town's Old Common Burial Ground, which I knew had grave markers tracing back to 1764. Main Street was deserted as I hiked across the shimmering pavement toward the wrought-iron gate. The rain had tapered into perfect damp-air graveyard-ambling conditions. Streetlights cut the pitchy darkness enough for me to pick my way past the thin stones, askew and so weathered that they were almost illegible. Tombstones like these are my absolute favourite, with their uniform shapes, orangey-green moss, engraved skulls, and old-world font.

The ground steamed as I passed beneath the long arms of each fat oak, deeper and deeper into the thicket of graves. I probed my mind for fear and found none. *Is something wrong with me*, I wondered? *Shouldn't I be worried that I'm about to be eaten by a Thriller-esque corpse, newly emerged from the dirt with a hurt on for fresh flesh?*

"No," I whispered, "I like it here." The silence, the permeation of eternal rest and relaxation, the absence of anxiety that us living seem to carry around in some kind of electrically charged force field, it all led me to a deep and peaceful place.

Two ghost stories drifted into my consciousness. The first, a late scene in *Rockbound*, involved a visit from a devil figure, who appears to David's only friend, the lightkeeper Gershom Born. The sopping wet apparition whispers his message to Gershom one night when David has fallen asleep, urging Gershom to exact revenge on Uriah for hoodwinking his love interest. Returning home in a pea-soup fog, Gershom steers Uriah and his son Casper toward "De Bull," a ripsnorting, boat-crushing shoal. Uriah's last words are "Sheer off, ye crazy loon," but Gershom ignores him, a maniacal look in his usually kind eyes. They all go down together.

The second was Joshua Slocum's run-in with the ghost captain of Columbus's famous ship, the *Pinta*. Battling food poisoning and a roiling sea, Slocum describes a painful night of writhing on his cabin floor, unable to steer the *Spray* in the squall. He is shocked to see a shaggy black-whiskered sailor towering above him. "You did wrong, Captain," the man says, "to mix cheese with plums." Slocum knew he was hallucinating, but he put full confidence in the spectral navigator and, shockingly, woke the next morning to find the *Spray* had held her course, chewing up ninety miles in the process.

When I keyed into the deserted inn, my fearless cemetery explorer mood dissipated a touch. Just behind the main door was another leading to the lobby, but that one was locked and the whole first floor was dark. I climbed the wooden stairs to the hallway and decided, spontaneously, to pass my door and explore the other passages that led off at dimly lit, crooked angles. If there were other guests, they were slumbering hard, because all I heard was the squeak of floor planks as I took each step.

A short stairway brought me to a kind of half floor with an upper landing that ended at a squat, five-foot door. "That's not a room," I whispered, "maybe the attic?"

As I got closer, I noticed something that made my pulse quicken: the deadbolt was out, and it rested on the frame. I could enter if I so pleased. A distant memory of *The Shining* misted into my mind, but I shrugged it off and inched nearer to the door, easing it open to reveal a black hole lit only by a distant striped light that I took to be a gable end.

I drew a deep breath. Long duckboard-style planks ran down a dusty path through the exposed roof trusses, each one with its own heat pump. *Okay*, I thought, *not too scary*. Pink blown-in insulation filled the darker cavities, and I kicked it aside as I walked slowly away from the door behind me.

I was hoping for an interesting attic full of old seafaring antiques, but all I found was a fifties-era hair-curling machine that resembled an Airstream trailer stood vertically. I coughed when I read its label: The Turbinator. Not the kind of relic I expected to find, but fascinating nonetheless. Thinking of cotton-candy hairstyles broke the spell for me, and I turned back down the planks with fresh resolve to bury myself in an actual bed.

As I passed the attic threshold and went to pull the door behind me, I felt something pass by, a gust of air that animated every follicle on my body. I froze. Ahead of me, leading down the carpeted corridor, was a wispy trail of pink insulation, so close to footprints that I almost screamed.

PART TWO

BLUENOSE
GHOSTS

Chapter 5

AFTER THE FLOOD

Where there has been sudden death
there is likely to be a return of the spirit.
—— *Bluenose Ghosts*

Larry, like his swirling brothers and sisters before him, moved on. Hurricanes always do. But they leave gifts in their wake. Powerful, beautiful, finite gifts. Gifts that turn surfers into agitated fiends willing to throw everything aside to open them up.

That morning I'd received a directive from the Surf Gods to execute a mission to catch Larry's last waves in a remote spot. I mapped out a day's ride from my room in Liverpool to Kejimkujik Seaside Adjunct, a national park forty kilometres south. When I got there an exhausting four hours later and learned that the ocean was a two-kilometre walk from the parking lot, my mission expanded to a twenty-four hour "hike-surf-camp strike," my favourite kind. I would have to strip the Ox, pack only the essentials, lug my gear down the trail, and find a home base. My surfer brain said, "Just go," but my teacher brain said, "Make a checklist." So I compromised by quickly sketching out what I knew I'd need for a night in the unknown wilds of Keji Seaside.

Balance was key, so I envisioned carrying a four-litre water jug in my left hand and the Tombstone under my right arm. My dry bag would have to hold the rest. Ground coffee and French press, stove and fuel, dried meal and can of Zoodles, plate and cutlery set, wetsuit and booties, hammock tent and sleeping bag, poncho-as-towel-slash-pillow, toothpaste and brush, notebook and pen. The straight goods, that's it.

I took each item off my makeshift Tombstone staging table and stuffed it in my pack. Checking the boxes felt good, though it gave me flashbacks of the daily to-do list I live on while teaching. If there's one quality most teachers share, it's a penchant for being hyper-organized. Survival depends on it.

And there, in the national park gravel lot on a clear afternoon, my checklist made me feel a bit like Joshua Slocum as he prepared to sail away from yet another port. He was legendary for having his shit together; I aspired to be his protégé.

As I finished my preparations, a few curious hikers passed by. They couldn't quite square my bike, board, and bag full of gear. One lady stepped up and strafed me with questions in a staccato Jersey Shore accent. "Where ya going? Ya plan to surf? Where'd ya come from? Are ya crazy?" as her husband stood back and looked distracted, clearly accustomed to his wife's insatiable curiosity.

I fended her off in the kindest way possible, but I stopped short of telling her how I'd left Liverpool in board shorts to become one with the pouring rain, how I'd been humiliated by an insanely long hill leaving Queensland Beach, how I'd navigated a stretch of the main 103 Highway by lying flat on my handlebars to keep control of the Ox as it got windswept, over and over, by thundering transport trucks. By the time her husband dragged her away, I'd reached my daily social quota. An evening on an isolated beach seemed even more necessary.

Chickadees dashed back and forth as I humped my gear along the crusher-dust path, careful not to slip in the fresh pools of rainwater. Spruce tunnel gave way to coastal barrens blanketed in rust-coloured ferns and thick gorse bush. The full water jug counterbalanced the Tombstone nicely and I trudged on at a decent clip, smiling at the few day trippers hiking the other way.

An occasional *Beware of Bears* sign grabbed my attention, but I was too focused on making the beach to register them. The sky was vivid blue for the first time in days, and I angled my face at the sun to burn off the slime of dampness I'd acquired on the morning's ride. By the time I made the first overlook bench, I collapsed on rubber legs like a world's strongest man competitor post-deadlift.

Two thoughts hit me when I took in the view: this place is stunning and...this place might be unsurfable right now. A constellation of granite boulders crowded the shoreline, ending at a long crescent beach fringed by seagrass dunes. Glassy green waves smashed the rocks and sent up jets of spray, a big decibel symphony of energetic collision. My lizard surf brain made quick calculations: rocks, rocks, everywhere rocks, and not a wave to surf? Unless I was willing to pay the price of course, which seemed to be a dull thud of body into a cold slab of God's finest immovable objects.

But the waves seemed to clean up way down the rock-studded shore, shaping lines that broke big and boomy, their crests feathering back in walls of offshore spray. I knew it was my only chance. Every hike-surf-camp strike mission demands flexibility and the acknowledgement that some unseen and unsurfed places were meant to stay that way. I vowed not to make a rash decision.

The rash decision I *did* make was camp-related.

As the wide trail gave way to a winding cobblestone footpath through a maze of ocean-smoothed shoreline mini-canyons, I scanned the scraggly trees for hammock options. The phrase "few and far between" was, I believe, coined by a hammock tenter. Not many options on the Keji beach, that's for sure.

I was enjoying my turn as Robinson Crusoe though, and I marvelled at the stunning rivulets of sand left by thousands of small spherical rocks embedded all along the low-tide beach. At one point, I shrugged off my load to guzzle water and spied a clean right-hand wave breaking off the last clump of rocks before the mess of closed-out beach break beyond. It looked surfable, maybe, as long as I stayed well clear of the rocks. Assuming I could make the bruising paddle-out through the frothing whitewash, that is.

A copse of stone-dead trees between the fringed dune and the high-tide line looked to be my best—my only?—option. I hastily ruled the

clumps of seaweed as a kind of safe tide boundary and got to work string-
ing the hammock up between the only two spruces with the correct
distance between them. Aside from a few snapped branches to allow
my line anchors to find purchase, I did not disturb the spot. This was a
stroke of luck. Solid dead trees that could hold a true load.

By the time I had my deluxe accommodations readied, an army
of clouds had invaded the late afternoon sky. The full-roar ocean did
the opposite of beckon me as I set up my stove next to my Tombstone-
turned-dining-room-table and boiled water for my dehydrated satchel, a
fragrant mush that could only generously be called pad Thai. A glance
back at my encampment made me laugh. It looked like a parachutist had
landed on a giant porcupine.

After a digestive stroll down the sand, I pulled on my wetsuit, waxed
up the Tombstone, and turned to face Larry's energy conduit and my
undisputed master, the vast Atlantic.

Some paddle-outs are easier than others, as any surfer knows. On
mellow summer days, you can glide out between sets and take your
place in the line-up with completely dry hair. Paddle-outs like that are
meditative in quality, allowing the mind to wander and the senses to
expand. You might hear a flock of cormorants flap past, their wings
beating a steady *slap*. Or you might take a long look at a full morning
moon hanging like a Christmas tree ornament. Or, if you're like me,
you might scoop up a mouthful of brine that shocks your taste receptors
awake. Those paddle-outs are good for the soul.

But on days when a hurricane is out at sea tearing at the fabric of
physics, a paddle-out becomes a monumental challenge. As I stood alone
on the ribbons of ocean-smoothed granite, Tombstone tethered to my
right ankle, I understood that it would be an accomplishment to simply
get past the shorebreak. No poetry allowed. This would be a feat of
head-down brute force and dogged persistence in the face of flashing
doubt. From my entry point I saw I would have to make it through three
lines of persistent whitewater before reaching the promised land, each
line a kind of barrelling wall forcing me back to the beach.

I got in and started paddling, my arms in full whirligig mode, heading straight for the first mountain. *Smash!* I tried to duck dive the wave,

but I got hit square, popping up in the swirl to reorient myself for the next one. *Smash again!* This time I stayed upright and managed a few harried strokes in the melee. *Smash!* Frantic paddle. *Smash!*

After what seemed like an hour, but was likely five minutes, I took a quick moment to see where I was. The current coming off the rocky stretch had whisked me down the beach, and I was still in the smash zone. This was my make-or-break moment, one all surfers recognize. Alone in the churning foam, deafened by thundering waves, it took all my foolish pride to override the impulse to just let the next wave sweep me back to shore. I had to double down.

Another micro-eternity later, I made it to safety by digging up the glassy face of an onrushing overhead wave that threw me and the Tombstone vertical, feathered spray showering down as I landed with a *smack*. Out past the breaking waves, I took a moment to breathe and let the mountains of unbroken swell pass beneath me, one after the other. *This must be how Slocum felt in big seas*, I thought. Waves are navigable as long as they don't break on your boat. Seasickness-inducing, no doubt, but there's a kind of comfort in the rhythmic trough-to-crest rolling that comes in deeper waters. As I straddled the Tombstone and watched the clean corduroy lines pulse my way from the misty blue horizon, I almost forgot why I was out there.

"Right, time to catch one of these beasts," I said, psyching myself up. "One wave, just one wave."

When conditions are maxed out and there is, as surfers are wont to say, "a lot of water moving," a one-wave session is commonplace. I resigned myself to it. I knew that if I somehow managed to get swept up by one of these bottle-green monstrosities it was a one-way street back to the sand. I vowed to make it count, laid back down on the Tombstone, and cautiously inched toward the impact zone to find my freight train home.

The thing to be wary of was the euphemistically named "clean-up set," a group of roguish waves that break deeper and smother the line-up with froth. In the kind of crushing beach break on offer at Keji, if I got cleaned up I was done. I kept an eye on the horizon as I let a couple of waves run past me, studying the takeoff spot and gauging how fast

they peeled down the line. When I saw a distant stack of green towers
marching my way, I knew it was either catch one or get rumbled. The
dreaded clean-up set had arrived.

I paddled hard toward the waves, and as I met the first wall I spun
and took a few deep strokes. I knew I had it as I felt the heave, and I
sprang to my feet just in time to beat the crashing lip — *boom!* — and
I was off, hurtling shoreward on a tiny piece of foam that bucked and
bounded down the avalanching face. By taking off on an angle I stayed
ahead of the wash, and I could see that my wave was about to morph
from moving mountain to sheer-faced El Capitan. Nothing to do but
race toward destruction, so I took two speed-gathering pumps and
aimed my line at the pinch point.

This is the moment when a good surfer might find himself ensconced
in a tube of cascading water before shrieking out of the wave's barrel in
a blast of spit. Not me. As I crouched I saw another wave breaking in the
opposite direction, and before I could think *Close out*, I veered beachward
and Supermanned myself flat on the Tombstone as the world detonated
behind me.

Somehow I managed to stay on top of the insane rodeo bull, and the
next thing I knew I was flying forward in prone position. I jostled and
rattled to the shallows where I was pounded into the sand and wiped off
my board. When I finally came to rest on the hard beach, I staggered
to my feet and knew from the crunch of my teeth that I'd taken a mean
sandblasting.

"Thanks, Larry," I said, blinking through the sting. "You certainly
brought the goods."

Some days, surfing is like a hot-oil massage, others it's a back-alley
boxing match. I was punch-drunk and smiling when I got back to my
wooded cemetery to ready myself for a night of rest.

Exhaustion, relief, and thirst dominated my mental landscape as I
set about prepping my junk in a wash of purple light. I saw that the tide
had risen and run closer to my camp, and I'd calculated that high tide
would come just short of my clump of dead trees, so I acted accordingly,
laying the Tombstone under the hammock so I could leave my shoes and
socks within reach for a mid-night leak.

I hung my wet stuff in the branches and walked my dry bag down the beach to a clump of seagrass on the dune face. "Gotta be bear safe," I said, patting the bag before skipping back barefoot.

My only hygienic move was a hasty tooth brush, which I accomplished by dipping the bristles in my jug, scrubbing away, and rinsing with a jet of post-gargle water. My sand-crawling hair would have to stay feral.

As I set my shoes and socks neatly on the Tombstone and stepped from the tarp into the gash of my hammock, I thought, *Hey, this isn't so bad. I'm here in a dry sleeping bag with my headlamp and a good book, with front-row seats to a primordial ocean cacophony that will only be enhanced by these babies, my trusty orange earplugs.*

After my customary struggle to get the sleeping bag right, I settled in for a mental cool-down guided by Helen Creighton, the first person curious and brave enough to document Nova Scotia's supernatural streak.

"Forerunner" is an intriguing word. Slice it in half and you have its meaning: a person or thing that runs before others. In surfing, forerunners are the first pulses of a distant storm, indicator waves that promise more swell to follow. In the world of the spirit, a forerunner warns of something unsettling on the horizon, an unavoidable and often sinister event.

Before Helen Creighton learned what a forerunner was, she heard one. Days prior to the death of her eldest brother's wife, a card game was interrupted by three loud, distinct knocks. Everyone heard it, but no one could pinpoint the sound. The wall it came from, strangely, had no door. After a quick inspection, the card game continued. Helen Creighton let the episode fade in her memory, never linking the knocks to the death of her sister-in-law.

All over Nova Scotia, from Cape Breton to Yarmouth to Wolfville to Halifax, Helen Creighton heard similar tales of the classic forerunner from Bluenosers she spent her career documenting on an early tape recorder. When her host finished singing folk songs for the evening, talk often turned to the spiritual realm. Those card game knocks, she realized, "Were the three death knocks. These are heard in certain houses by certain people and they come as a warning of approaching death." Because she had first-hand experience with forerunners herself, Helen Creighton was particularly interested to see how common they were in the countryside.

Her writing style is direct. She asks a question and·stands aside. Take this interchange from the first chapter of *Bluenose Ghosts*:

> I remember how my breath stopped momentarily one day
> when Mr. Eddy Deal of Seabright finished the folk song
> he was recording for me and said, knowing my interest in
> such things, "Did you ever hear of a man walking with
> himself?" I said no, I hadn't. "Well, there was a man
> here," he continued, "who felt somebody walking beside
> him and when he looked, he realized it was his own appar-
> ition. He was so frightened that he couldn't speak, for he
> knew the belief that this was a forerunner of death. A few
> months later he died."

Seeing a vision of yourself, hearing boards being nailed up, rum-bling ghost wagons, *tap tap taps* of the coffin maker, doors opening on their own, drowned men walking on water, balls of fire, a bird in the house — these are just some of the forerunners Creighton's subjects spun yarns about. She was effective at collecting these stories because she genuinely believed that what she heard was the tale teller's truth. She herself admits to spending her twenties on a skeptical tack, holding no truck with the backwoods superstitions that ran rampant among the older generations. As Creighton aged, she decided to tune in to broader frequencies.

Bluenose Ghosts, published in 1957, captures the distant echoes of a world view that was quite common in the latter half of the nineteenth century. When the ideas of the Swedish mystic Emanuel Swedenborg, who claimed to communicate with spirits while awake, came into full flower, the public was ready to believe in the basic tenet of the fashion-able new religious movement known as Spiritualism.

It posits that spirits of the dead exist and have both the ability and the inclination to communicate with the living. Spiritualists even had a specific date to mark the beginning of their movement: March 31, 1848, the day Kate and Maggie Fox of Hydesville, New York, reported that they had contacted a spirit who communicated through rapping noises, audible to witnesses. Before they were debunked years later, the Fox sisters were the first celebrity mediums. Spirit rappings, automatic slate writing, table turning, trumpet mediumship, sealed-letter readings, spirit photography, and seances soon became popular forms of entertainment and catharsis. Powering the movement was a desperate need to connect with lost loved ones.

From our über-rational twenty-first-century vantage, the practices of spiritualism seem naïve and kitsch. Think Ouija boards and *Ghostbusters*. But it's worth considering that a who's who of scientists and intellectuals flirted with the practice, among them Nobel laureate Pierre Curie, evolutionary biologist Alfred Russel Wallace, and physicist Sir Oliver Lodge. Charles Dickens joined the Ghost Club, a collective focused on the scientific study of alleged paranormal activities. Even Thomas Edison drank the Kool-Aid: he tried to develop a "spirit phone," an ethereal device that could record the voices of the dead. Investigating the spirit world was serious business back then. By 1897, Spiritualism claimed to have eight million followers worldwide.

Its most prominent booster was Sir Arthur Conan Doyle, creator of the world's favourite fictional detective, Sherlock Holmes. The carnage of World War One and the loss of his son, Kingsley, bolstered his interest in contacting spirits. In 1926, he published a fat, two-volume book called *The History of Spiritualism*, just as practices like spirit rapping and seances were falling out of favour to make way for stunt magician Harry Houdini, who began packing houses with shows trumpeting headlines like "Do Spirits Return? Houdini says NO—and Proves It."

Supernatural currents stayed electrified in Nova Scotia long after. Descendants of German and Celtic backgrounds made sure of it. Helen Creighton spent twenty-eight years gathering a wealth of material from every corner, tempering it all with the assurance, "I do not suggest that all stories are actually true." Her candour stands out, but it's her openness to the unknown and unprovable that informs her classic book. Isn't it the supreme hubris of our species to say that anything outside our sensory perception doesn't actually exist?

"I have heard it argued that a ghost story is of little value," Creighton writes, "unless it can be substantiated, but how can you prove something that has taken place only once and may never occur again? For myself I consider well the integrity of the informant, if he is temperate in his habits, and how much his outlook upon life has been coloured by a superstitious environment."

Wham!

A hard knock to the back of my head ripped me from a black sleep. As confused as I was in that strange, shocking moment, I knew in my core that this was no dream. This was a physical truth — something hit me. Hard.

As my consciousness floated back to the surface, I tried to sit up, a laughable thing to attempt in a hammock tent. My first thought was *bear.* Maybe a bear had swiped at me, hoping I'd fall out like candy from a breached piñata.

"Oh my God," I whispered. This was no time to stay put; I had to get out no matter what. In a panic I fumbled to find the Velcro seam — *rrrrip* — and what I saw outside sent me for another mental tailspin. Where was my board? Why were my shoes so far away? Something about the moonlit landscape looked off. I swung my feet out and planted them on the sand, ducking down to emerge in a tense crouch, my arms out in an absurd protective gesture. The ground was damp and rock-hard. I scanned the stand of dead trees for the bear I would have to wrestle, Leo DiCaprio style. But nothing stirred.

Utter, middle-of-the-night confusion swirled in my brain. What the hell had punched me in the head? Could my evening with Helen Creighton have brought a haunting about? Was it the ghost of Joshua Slocum, come to deliver me a crucial message?

I clued in, finally, when I registered a wetness on my hindquarters that I knew was not the result of a bladder blowout. I reached back in the tent for my headlamp. The beam of light confirmed it: I'd been swamped by a storm surge. My shoes were sopping and filled with sand, the Tombstone had flipped and wedged between two seaweedy branches. Sure enough, the roaring ocean was much closer, maybe only six metres away and resolutely frothing under a blanket of winking stars.

I slapped my forehead and cursed under my breath. Here I was, masquerading as some kind of waterman, and I somehow forgot about what *always* happens when there's a big swell. I'd witnessed dozens of storm surges back in Cow Bay, days when the causeway was impassible because the ocean was tossing rocks clear over the top, strewing the road with debris. It was the Tombstone that had slammed me awake, I knew it. The surge ran up so fast that the board was launched skyward, its rail kissing my skull before floating off in the receding wash, which had to be at least a metre deep based on the state of my swamped buns. I stood there like some lost coal miner with my mouth open. There was nothing left to do but laugh.

I unhooked my water jug from a snapped branch and took a swig to clear my thoughts. Now that I was awake, I needed a plan. Back behind the beach was a brutish world filled with bears, so that was a no go. I knew I had to stick it out on the sand. After pacing around, I convinced myself that the surge was a one-off, max high-tide thing, and my best bet to make it through the long night was to simply get back in the hammock and try to fall asleep again. Sure, my sleeping bag would be soaked, but the night was warm enough and I'd slept wet before. That was it, my elegant solution.

After collecting my stuff and stashing it at the crest of the dune, I got back in the cursed cocoon. One, two, three minutes passed without incident as I convinced my body to ignore my wet midsection. I breathed slowly, in and out. It had to be a rogue wave. The worst was over and the tide would drop from there. Nothing to do but try to sleep. I felt myself slipping back under, miraculously, when a truly heinous thing happened. I got sloshed, again.

This time my whole sleeping bag was submerged, and a disturbing weightlessness took over, a disgusting sensation akin to a human teabag being dipped in a salty soup. It wasn't panic this time but more of a disappointed resignation that led me to rip open the Velcro and take a look.

A roiling stew of sandy water flooded the stumps, pulling back with urgency whatever seaweed it contained. I just waited it out; what else could I do? Much jaw clenching and snorting followed as I came to grips with my new reality, namely that I was spending my fine post-surf night literally *in* the ocean. Ten minutes later I got swamped for a third and final time, right up to the armpits. It's best that the roar of the waves drowned out the once-in-a-lifetime shame cackle that emerged, involuntarily, from my throat.

It was official. I had been punked, not by Slocum's ghost or Poseidon or Neptune or even God, but by that most reverent and all-powerful grand dame, Mother Nature herself.

The last gasp of any hurricane swell is benign, a sweet farewell kiss on the cheek of every surfer who dared to tango. The whirling dervish continues on past Newfoundland and into the North Atlantic to bring the goods to surfers from Iceland to Morocco. Those last, often gentle pulses from the storm rings coincide with a sense of deep exhalation. Before the day's sea breeze kicks up, a surfer is wise to paddle out for a few golden offshore beauties. At Keji-by-the-Sea, I was lucky enough to man-hug Larry before full oceanic stillness descended.

The spot I'd surfed just fourteen hours earlier looked much more inviting, each backlit emerald wave a smaller and more organized version of its previous beast-mode self. Now that I'd earned my tide intel the hard way, I knew I had a couple of hours to surf and pack up for the hike back to my stashed Ox and the open road. I suited up with a growing need for redemption.

After an easy paddle out, I rested on the Tombstone, letting the waves pass below. A thought of sharks flashed up, but I snubbed it. As the sun hoisted off the sea's surface, I promised myself that I would learn a life lesson from my brush with the flood tide. Like Slocum says, read the ocean, know its action, respect its power, be humble in the face of its blessings and dangers. Sharks are a minuscule risk; much more destructive is our tendency to underestimate the ocean.

The coil inside me released after a few fun waves, little green runners with blown back crests of whitewater jewels, and I came out of the surf with renewed buoyancy.

As I hopped along the sand, a configuration of black-and-white speckled rocks drew my eye. Three golf ball–sized spheres, right there in a perfect triangle. I knew I was looking at my family: Genny, Hazel, and Rosalie. I bent down to pick them up, and I felt the sun warm me through my wetsuit. I was burnt out, windswept, thirsty, and genuinely happy. Gratitude for what I had welled up, a much more comforting surge, and all I could think to say, to whoever might be receptive to my signal, was "Thank you."

Chapter 6

THE DOORS

Something outside is helping me all the time.
Haven't you felt it too?
—— *Bluenose Ghosts*

The Shelburne Guild Hall Market was pumping when I pulled up on the Ox and planted my numb feet on gravel. After running solo for such a long stretch, the prospect of joining a horde of locals was intimidating, so I opted to start with a peripheral lurk before homing in on my objective, which was not the purchase of a beeswax candle or artisanal stained glass. Sustenance was my prey; I was raging with hunger once more.

A stiff wind cut the generous sun, forcing the squinty vendors to anchor their tablecloths with any weights they could find. Ignoring the artists and essential oil merchants, I quickly mapped out a route for my belly-filling mission. Two baked-goods spots here and here, coffee there, a guy grilling sausages back there, and some beauty picnic tables tucked under trees beside musicians over there. As I hobbled around the margins, I passed a table set back from the others and made eye contact with a young woman wearing a mushroom hat and a V-shaped chain on her forehead, a purple amulet shining between her eyes. She smiled and I smiled back, but my atrophied conversation skills kept my feet moving, bringing me home to the Ox after a favourable circumnavigation.

Something told me I should go talk to the smiling woman, but I shrugged it off and poured my last ounce of energy into purchasing, in quick succession, a chocolate-dipped oat cake, a sauerkraut-loaded sausage, and a large black coffee, which I proceeded to unceremoniously inhale next to the musician tent. The jam was led by a lady in a red vest and blue blocker sunglasses on a bongo drum, followed intently by a backup ensemble of two elderly men on acoustic guitars, a toe-tapping accordion man, and a young bearded guy on Casio keyboard. The grassy spot jumped with little kids and grandparents spinning and laughing and busting out wholly original dance moves.

After guzzling a litre of water and basking in the sun, I found the courage to circle back and approach the mushroom-hat woman.

"Hi there," I said as I stepped up to the table. It was draped in a deep purple tapestry with a bright green butterfly embroidered under the word "feral."

"Hello!" she said. "Welcome to Feral Chocolate and Herbals. I'm Crystal."

"I'm Ryan," I replied. "Wow, this looks interesting."

The table was covered with small paintings, jars of homemade kombucha, green cardboard containers full of glowing yellow chanterelle mushrooms, and a pyramid arrangement of hand-wrapped chocolate bars as centrepiece.

"We make everything ourselves from ingredients we harvest on our land," she said, her blue eyes wide. "The chocolate is all natural...is there anything you're interested in?"

Resisting the urge to say "All of it," I said, "I definitely have to try the chocolate."

While she took me through my options, I had the distinct feeling that this was no average farmer's market stall, and that Crystal was no stranger to the mystical side of existence. The Willy Wonka undertones were potent. Once I'd made my choice—a cardamom-infused bar wrapped with hand-stamped paper—Crystal leaned closer and whispered, "We also make psilocybin chocolate."

I looked up and stared at her third eye, then back to her actual eyes, black pupils dominating blue.

"They're not up here," she said, waving her arm over the table, "but I've got a couple tucked away. I get the sense you'd be interested."

"I am...," was my response, but it felt as if someone else said it.

Her smile widened. "This one," she said, bringing a road map–wrapped bar into view, "this one's what we call a Starseed Bar. We find the chocolate enhances the experience. Have you tried psilocybin before?"

"Um," I thought back. "Yes, yes I have, once or twice." At my bachelor party over a decade back a friend had pulled out a bag of mushrooms, and I'd taken part, though the memory was vague.

"This one has three grams of powdered psilocybin infused. It's a Golden Teacher variety."

"Wait, did you say...Golden Teacher?" I whisper-hissed, my pulse racing.

"Yes, Golden Teacher," she said, "known for its ability to open up those philosophical doors."

I stayed quiet. A wave of serendipity crested in my brain.

"But make sure you're cautious," Crystal said, "hunker down for a few hours, five or six at least. You should be in a safe place. Make sure you feel comfortable."

"Right," I said, "of course."

Before I could register what had happened, I'd paid Crystal, adding a mason jar of kombucha, and we'd parted ways, her luminous eyes and hippie aura floating me back to the Ox.

"What have I done?" I muttered under my breath. *Did I just buy magic mushrooms at the Shelburne Farmer's Market?* I laid the rectangular bar on the Tombstone and flipped it over to find an ingredients sticker holding the folded map paper together. Here's what it said:

Starseed Bar
Ingredients: Cacao Butter, Cocoa Powder (50% Raw / 50% Amber #3),
Coconut Oil, Maple Syrup (NS), Honey (NS), Sea Salt (NS), Chili Pepper,
Vanilla (pure), 3 grams of Powdered psilocybin cubensis
* A Golden Teacher Variety *

*All ingredients organic, dairy free, non GMO. Proudly made in the
hills of NS. Free yer mind & yer ass will follow!!!*

I stifled a laugh and looked around suspiciously, slipped the contraband into my handlebar treasure chest and zipped it closed, mounted the Ox once more, and pondered when the right moment might be to take Crystal's invitation and embark on my trip to the Chocolate Factory.

Twenty-four hours earlier, I'd left Keji with the juice for some serious road carnage. The gravel hills leading back to Highway 103 had other ideas of course, and I soon had to resign myself to the slow, grinding pace demanded by my trusty-not-swift Ox.

With a run of fair weather ahead, I knew I'd traded cold and wet for warm and buggy, so I slathered on my SPF 50, spritzed on the DEET, and made sure my water bottle was topped up. From Port Joli to Sable River I had no choice but to merge into the ripping current of those combustion rapids they call "the 103." Dropping in, I cowered back into my paved-shoulder crouch and prayed these drivers would have mercy on the Ox and I.

The hilly run was unremarkable, except for one stunning display of late-stage masculinity. As I crested a rise just past Granite Village, a thundering sound tensed me up. It was an oncoming parade of Harley-Davidson motorcycles. The front man sat back in his black leathers as if he were sitting in a La-Z-Boy watching Sunday afternoon football, vintage pilot goggles and World War Two–era helmet framing his bearded ZZ Top face. Directly behind him came seven more hogs of similar ilk, each rider a model of stoicism, owning the road in full snowbird formation.

I was awestruck for some reason, so I risked an exuberant wave, flapping my left arm from windmill to peace sign to military salute. Not one of those badasses waved back. When the last guy roared by, his legs splayed out in stirrups like he was going down a waterslide, I felt jilted.

As a kid, I loved motorcycles, spending my free time dirt biking the fields behind our house. Now that my allegiance was to the hard-earned pedal, however, the absurdity of an eight-man, limp-wrist-powered fly-by hit home.

Combustion is pathetic, I realized. It gets you places easily, sure, but what does it take away from your human experience? I had a taste of the bitterness Slocum must have felt when he saw those steamboats churn past his schooner, their stacks spewing black. Really though, I was probably just disappointed no one waved to me.

The Starseed Bar curveball, and its promise of a future psychedelic experience, should have lifted my spirits, but it had the opposite effect. After the market, I walked the sleepy streets of Shelburne drained of enthusiasm, scoping each quiet corner for a potential hammock spot. Across from a row of fading century homes I found a cemetery with an open corner under foliage, but it repelled me. I wasn't ready to cast my lot in with the dead.

Maybe I need a salad, I thought, so I trudged up to the Sobeys and bought one with more plastic wrapping than lettuce. Next door at the Lawtons pharmacy I found an ancient payphone that only took quarters, broke a ten-dollar bill, picked up the receiver, and was told by a kind voice that it would be eight dollars for the first minute to call our Cow Bay number. I hung up.

The insult to injury came when I learned that not only did Lawtons not carry calling cards, but also the friendly teenager didn't know what a calling card was.

"I'm old," I told him, and a mirror behind the counter confirmed it: my haggard face was wreathed in mostly grey hair. I'd honestly thought it was brown before I left Cow Bay.

It was decision time. Squat in some sketchy corner of Shelburne or move into parts unknown. On my map, I noticed a green inverted *V* across the harbour from Shelburne's waterfront and decided that The Islands Provincial Park would offer my best chance at a secure night, even if it broke my vagabond code.

The sky's blue went mute grey as I jumped through the self-registration hoops. The park was empty except for two RVs near the entrance, so I had the run of the place, and I chose a site in the centre that immediately made me feel better. No neighbours, ideally spaced trees, an actual picnic table and—yessir—a firepit with a bent grill over it.

"I need a fire," I said to the darkening forest. I'd done without camp-fires up to then, mainly to keep a low profile, but now it felt like my life depended on huddling close to a roaring fire, smoking my pipe and reading more from *Bluenose Ghosts*. After a methodical camp set-up, I ran for firewood and got my blaze going full blast. The heat melted every ounce of melancholy away, and soon I was puffing on my pipe like some sailor home from a gale, feet up, pretending that this was my hearth.

Helen Creighton's book glowed in my hands. I wasn't convinced that ghosts exist, or that the dead can speak to the living, but she made a solid case for trusting my senses, for embracing my conduits to "something outside."

A slashing rain lengthened the long uphill from The Islands park to the Black Loyalist Heritage Centre in Birchtown. That whole morning, Jessie, a short, no-nonsense woman with tightly braided hair, humoured me as I walked around the empty museum in soaked board shorts and flip-flops, reading every single scrap of information I could find.

I'd assailed her with questions after scrolling through a detailed time-line of the African experience from ancient times to 1792, when half of the Black Loyalists who'd been granted land in Birchtown a decade earlier took the offer to sail to Sierra Leone to found the city known as Freetown. At first, Jessie seemed annoyed, but after a while she walked me through the fateful decision of her forebears to accept an offer from the British to leave the newly formed United States in exchange for a piece of land and their freedom. She got fired up when I asked about the 1784 Shelburne Race Riots, which I was shocked to find out were North America's first.

"White settlers couldn't find work," she said, her pace quickening, "so they took their anger out on the Black Loyalists, burning their homes and chasing them out of Shelburne." She shook her head emphatically.

After Jessie doused my last flames of curiosity with facts, I headed over to the Anglican church to read more informational signs. When I came out, she was there again, this time cross-legged and lighting a smoke. I shielded my eyes from the post-rain sun and waved hello.

She introduced me to her cousin, Sherry, who said, "We're first cousins, both descendants of the first Black settlers in Birchtown, but look at me. I got red hair and blue eyes, ha! Surprises anyone who don't know their Black history."

I asked the question that had been gnawing at me for hours. "Have either of you ever had any run-ins with ghosts here?"

"Ghosts?" Sherry replied, pulling animatedly on her smoke and exhaling a plume in my direction. "Oh yes indeed, plenty a' ghost stories around here, my love. A couple years back I heard one singin' in the church and went to investigate — they sometimes sing in there — and somethin' brushed right past me, true story. But ya gotta ask Jessie here about her daughter. She's got some doozies."

Jessie jumped in after a chuckle. "Yes, yes, my daughter grew up here, and she always said there were lots of ghosts around. One time, when she was twelve or so, a spirit woke her up, and she followed him out in the pouring rain to help him find his drowned wife. Never scared, she was. Never. Always felt like ghosts needed her help."

Just as I was about to mention Slocum's ghost, Sherry called out, "Darryl! Darryl, come over here!"

A man in coveralls materialized. "Whaa?"

"Darryl," coaxed Sherry, "tell this young fella yer ghost story."

My head spun as Darryl launched into a harrowing tale about the time he came across a woman in a green coat by the railway tracks standing still, and how he'd described her to his friend later and how his friend had casually replied, "Oh, that's just my grandmother. She's been dead for twenty years."

"Can't explain it," Darryl said, taking off his sweat-stained hat, "but I know what I saw."

"Tell ya what," Jessie added as she stubbed out and stood up, "when my husband died I knew his spirit was still in the house, plain as day. The bugger would knock down the china when I was asleep! Even turned on a light with no batteries in it, swear to God."

"So there ya have it," Sherry said, "plenty a' ghost stories here. Creepy, maybe, but not scary. Just have to shoo 'em out sometimes."

With that, the cigarette break was over, and I was alone again, my mind a swirl of smoke and mirrors. As I emerged back on the road, a fine mist rose from the warming asphalt. I pointed the Ox in a direction I felt confident would lead to a safe place in solitude, maybe even safe enough to experiment with the expansion of my consciousness.

What do Aldous Huxley, Michael Pollan, and Mike Tyson have in common? If you said facial tattoos, you'd be off the mark. All three of them could accurately be labelled a "psychonaut," or someone who has experimented with psychedelic substances to explore their mind, and in the case of Mike Tyson, to heal.

Huxley, famed author of the dystopian classic *Brave New World*, was one of the first prominent intellectuals to undergo a controlled ingestion of a psychedelic substance — in his case mescaline, the active principle of the sacred cactus known as peyote — and report his findings. His radical essay *The Doors of Perception* (first published in 1954) is written in a stunningly sober style. Before the gonzo prose of Ken Kesey, Tom Wolfe, and Hunter S. Thompson, there was Huxley's buttoned-up tweed scientific report, which carries this famous line: "Thus it came about that, one bright May morning, I swallowed four-tenths of a gramme of mescalin dissolved in half a glass of water and sat down to wait for the results."

As we journey with Huxley away from everyday consciousness, we find ourselves staring at the pleats of Huxley's corduroy pants, seeing patterns more beautiful than any grand cathedral. A small team of scientists ask him questions along the way and eventually take him outside, where he is floored by the rapturous beauty of a red peony. He found that "the mind was primarily concerned, not with measures and locations, but with being and meaning." This was "out there" stuff for the 1950s public, and in some corners Huxley was unfairly labelled a heretic, a drug pusher looking to corrupt the minds of the youth. Really, though,

Huxley was simply a curious scientist doing what he did best: conducting an experiment.

As mentioned in J.G. Ballard's introduction to *The Doors of Perception*, the experiment was founded on a fascinating hypothesis that "despite the wonders of human consciousness, Huxley believed that our brains have been trained during the evolutionary millennia to screen out all those perceptions that do not directly aid us in our day to day struggle for existence." The resulting six-hour trip changed Huxley; he had a mystical experience, one that stayed with him and altered his outlook on life. "The man who comes back through the Door in the Wall," he wrote, "will never be quite the same as the man who went out."

Michael Pollan, the American immersion journalist, dug deep for his 2018 psychic travelogue with a seriously long subtitle: *How to Change Your Mind: What the New Science of Psychedelics Teaches Us About Consciousness, Dying, Addiction, Depression, and Transcendence.* He burrows deep into the cultural history of psychedelic plants, reminding us that "for our species, plants and fungi with the power to radically alter consciousness have long and widely been used as tools for healing the mind, for facilitating rites of passage, and for serving as a medium for communicating with supernatural realms, or spirit worlds." He highlights the serious scientific research of the 1950s and early '60s and laments the abuse and eventual vilification of psychedelics from the later '60s on, when grants were pulled, research was halted, and scientists shied away from the controversial topic. Plant-based psychedelic research went underground.

Pollan clued in when he read a 2010 story by John Tierney in the *New York Times* headlined "Hallucinogens Have Doctors Tuning In Again." It outlined research experiments that gave large doses of psilocybin to terminal cancer patients in an attempt to help them cope with the "existential distress" of their looming death. Johns Hopkins, UCLA, and New York University took part in the study. Pollan was intrigued by the findings. "Many of the volunteers," he writes in *How To Change Your Mind*, "reported that over the course of a single guided psychedelic 'journey' they reconceived how they viewed their cancer and the prospect of dying. Several of them said they had lost their fear of death completely. The reasons offered for this transformation were intriguing but also somewhat elusive. 'Individuals transcend their primary identification with their bodies and experience ego-free states,' one of the researchers was quoted as saying. They 'return with a new perspective and profound acceptance.'"

Pollan is careful, of course, to warn people that this kind of experimentation should only be done in controlled settings and never by anyone prone to psychotic episodes. It's all about "set" and "setting," he learned. "Set is the mind-set or expectation one brings to the experience," he writes, "and setting is the environment in which it takes place."

The first-person experimentation that drives *How To Change Your Mind* was set in motion when Pollan read a peer-reviewed psychopharmacology paper that "demonstrated that a high dose of psilocybin could be used to safely and reliably 'occasion' a mystical experience — typically described as the dissolution of one's ego followed by a sense of merging with nature or the universe." Following in the footsteps of pscychonaut scientists like Huxley before him, Pollan knew the only path to a full understanding of the potential benefits of psilocybin was to try it himself. So, in a pre-staged clinical setting, he munched the mushrooms and let go of his psychic controls.

The proof of his experimentation is in the pudding: he titled his book *How to Change Your Mind*. Pollan's cautiously optimistic tone pulled psychedelics back into the medical mainstream, catching the attention of many, including iconoclastic heavyweight boxer Mike Tyson.

"Everyone thought I was crazy," Tyson told Reuters in a 2021 piece by Rory Carroll. "I bit this guy's ear off! I did all this stuff, and once I got introduced to the shrooms...my whole life changed. To think where I was — almost suicidal — to this now. Isn't life a trip, man? It's amazing medicine, and people don't look at it from that perspective."

Tyson's experience with psilocybin led him to invest in Wesana Health, a first of its kind company dedicated to studying the fungi's ability to treat traumatic brain injury in athletes, veterans, and others. Wesana ran a clinical research project with the World Boxing Council to examine the potential of psilocybin to help boost the brain health of boxers. Tyson goes big with his praise of plant-based psychedelics, saying, "Proper therapeutic use could help create a more empathetic and just society. I believe this is good for the world."

Aldous Huxley, Michael Pollan, and Mike Tyson carefully eased their doors of perception open with positive results. I knew I'd never get a facial tattoo, so maybe a psychedelic experience was the next best thing. Something told me I'd find a clue, a hint, a vapour trail, a taste of the mist shrouding Slocum's sails.

The hills are heinous, long and steep
But I have promises to keep
And miles to go before I speak
And miles to go before I freak

That riff on Robert Frost, among many other spontaneous thought volcanoes, fuelled my progress along the hilly shoreline of Shelburne Harbour. I turned the crank over and over as the Ox and I chugged through Churchover, Gunning Cove, Carleton Village, Roseway, and Round Bay, all sleepy rural spots within striking distance of a string of world-class white-sand beaches.

Working a hot tip I received from a local woman at the Irving station, I turned down an unmarked road and bumped along on beach stone, dodging deep puddles as the forest grew thicker and more stunted. As promised, after a meandering downhill, I came to an opening that spit me out on a wide expanse of back beach dune, where the Ox got promptly and properly stuck in the sand. A quick exploratory dash had me hopping with joy: I'd found my desert-island beach spot.

The kilometre-long sandy crescent stretched to a cobble point on both sides, with single dwellings visible on each head like two lonely sentinels. Easygoing waves lapped at the shore, and the sun's angle spoke of 3:00 p.m., give or take. Being a Monday, and judging from the lack of fresh tire tracks, I deduced that I would have the beach to myself for the rest of the day and overnight. The "setting" for my Starseed experiment seemed ideal. And, as far as I could tell, my mind "set" felt stable. Fantastical, prone to imaginative outbursts, free of any societal moors, yes, but stable nonetheless.

"This is my window," I said to the gulls studding a ridge of seaweed.

The ensuing hour was a whirl of military-serious preparation. I marched back to the Ox, stripped all the gear off and extracted him from the quicksand, selected a semi-open spot between two trees engulfed in mossy old man's beard, strung up the hammock, separated my beach supplies, gathered the panniers and dry bag neatly under a tarp, and propped the Tombstone against a tree to mark the spot, officially, as "weird guy camp realm." The only commentary came from a spitting mad squirrel, his spicy chirps echoing through the quiet woods.

I took my handlebar box, my kitchen Tupperware, my jug of water, my poncho, towel, and sleeping bag and turned for the beach, where I laid everything out methodically, dropping a beach rock on each corner of the towel to keep it from flapping in the sea breeze. I had my food—a gas-station pizza twister—and my full water jug, so my basic human needs would be met. There was nothing left to do but pull out my notebook and Starseed Bar and lie down.

"This is a science experiment," I said, "so I should treat it as such." That meant laying out my lab-report headings in true middle-school science teacher style. Here's what I wrote down:

Statement of the Problem

I have a mystery mushroom chocolate bar, and I wonder what it will do to me.

Hypothesis

Within an hour, colours will get sharper and sounds more distinct. My head will start entertaining deeper thoughts that challenge my perception of reality. One truism will be revealed at least. I will be back to normal in about five hours, hopefully before bedtime.

Materials
- Golden Teacher psilocybin-infused chocolate bar
- Notebook and pen
- Food and water

For my Procedure, I gently unwrapped the bar, pulled it out and, realizing it was a melter, stuffed it in my face like Augustus Gloop in *Charlie and the Chocolate Factory.* "No turning back now," I said, my heart pounding in anticipation of the best part of any science experiment, the Results.

Nothing happened for the first half-hour, so I decided to take a bare-foot stroll to the southern end of the beach, whistling as I went. Wispy strands of white cloud sat motionless on land, leaving a wall of blue over the ocean. As I walked I took huge drafts of pungent salt air into my lungs and blew them out, dragon-style.

Near the spot where sand gave way to cobble headland, I crossed a running stream that drained an obscured salt marsh, and I halted in my tracks. The water was a rusty red colour and the snaking grooves it carved recalled the Grand Canyon.

"Beautiful," I said. A tinge of added importance had leaked into my thoughts, and I registered this as a forerunner of what was to come. The red river felt vitally important—not to my life, but to itself. "Hmm," I said, "very interesting."

Things escalated from there. On my walk back I perceived the thousands of beach stones as a mosaic of great artistic importance, as if the world was morphing into an immense art gallery. I would say something like "wow" and then laugh at myself for saying it, and I was overtaken by an urge to lay face down on my towel with my eyes closed. I did that for a bit, kneading sand with my toes, then I pulled out my road maps for an impromptu inspection. This cracked me up even more. I traced my finger down my route and started rattling off town names I'd be seeing in the coming days.

"Port Saxon," I said in a pompous English accent, laughing. "I grant thee...Port Saxon." Then "Coffinscroft," laughs, "Villagedale," laughs, "Riverhead," more laughs, and so on, until my eyes found "Shag

Harbour," and I couldn't take it anymore. Everything on the map was funny to me, almost too hilarious, so I sat up and took a big slug of water. It went down like a golden epiphany.

"Holy cow," I said, "this is working."

I had to go, had to move, so I stood back up and put my duct-taped sunglasses on, pulled my hat down low, and, sensing a chill in the air, draped my sleeping bag around me like a royal robe. If anyone saw me in that getup, they would have to conclude that I was either on the vanguard of modern fashion or it was Halloween. By then, I was completely assured of my solitude, allowing my mind to follow the whims of my dilated senses wherever they spun off.

"Hello, seagulls!" I said as I approached their roost on the now profound, lasagna-shaped seaweed. They flew around me in a wondrous formation and I knew they were my friends. Here I began a lively conversation with myself, asking questions and answering, stopping for long quizzical looks at footprints, clouds, and spackled rocks. When I returned to my towel, which had taken on the significance of a safe dwelling, I took out my pizza twister and tried a bite.

The pita bread felt like cardboard in my mouth, so I put it back, saying, "Looks like eating is a no go," to which I answered, "Yep, stick to the water."

I sat there for a long time talking, laughing, and watching the sky bleed from blue to mauve, feeling warm and happy. When I first heard the rumble of tires on cobblestone, I took it for distant thunder. "Interesting," I said. Then it came closer, and my mind clued in. "Oh no," I said, "other people!"

And indeed it was, in the form of a safari-beige Toyota truck, which pulled right up on the crest above me. I wouldn't call it panic, but the confusion that spread over me threatened to extinguish the calm I'd found, maybe forever.

Before I could hatch a plan, a bouncing dog flew from the truck straight for me, and my gut instinct was to embrace it, which I did, letting him frantically lick my face.

"Flint!" a voice called. "Down boy!"

"It's okay," I heard myself say, "I love dogs."

"Sorry about that," said the man as he loomed over me. "He's harmless."

Through my short-circuiting senses, I managed to stay sane as the man, his wife, and Flint started down the beach on their sunset walk. I took some deep breaths and tried to take stock of the situation. The beach looked darker, I felt colder, and my bubbly chatter was gone.

"Hold it together," I said, "they're only here for a walk. Hang in there."

I took a few more hits of water and sat back down, eyes closed, rehearsing what I might say when they got back. A curious quantity of time passed. When I chanced a look down the beach, they were right there, metres away, three dusky apparitions framed by an electric-blue sea. Flint flew at me again, but this time I was ready. I felt confident enough to attempt a conversation.

The friendly man, a retired conservation officer, introduced himself as Sandy.

"Saw yer set-up in the woods," he said.

"Oh, ya, that's me," I mumbled. "I'll be gone in the morning."

"I love it," he said. "I used to free camp all the time. I'd even do it in winter!"

"Wow, really?" I said, my wide-eyed exuberance flooding back in.

And so it went. By the end of our chat, Sandy's wife, Sharon, had taken a picture of us and texted it to Genny, whose number I rattled off in a lightning strike of memory. Turns out Sandy was an old sailor from way back, and his great-grandfather had been a clipper-ship captain in the same era as Joshua Slocum. Sandy even had an original copy of his great-grandfather's sailing logs, and soon I had plans to stop by Sandy's place in Port Clyde the next day for lunch and a yarn about Slocum. A brush with the man himself.

As I watched the truck's headlights pull back and disappear into the woods, I knew that a new phase of my Starseed exploration had begun, a phase of bundling up in my poncho and sleeping bag, pulling on my toque, and pacing the newly moonlit beach, back and forth, until the whole sky was speckled like a Jackson Pollock painting. Odd thoughts burbled up, crystal and honest, and I tried each one out aloud, bantering

with myself. The diamond thought was this phrase: "No one needs me."
I spoke it once, then again, each time with a new angle of understanding. My heart seemed full, and I felt so completely sure of my life's core,
which was Genny and the girls.

"No one needs me" wasn't about my family. "Of course they need
me, we need each other," I countered. "No one needs me . . . right now."
This was that oneness-with-the-universe vibe I'd read about. Free,
maybe inconsequential, but free, and so very fortunate to be on this
beach with that fat moon and those blazing stars.

I kept walking and I knew it would get no darker so I welcomed the
night. At once I realized the moon represented my mother and the biggest, brightest star in the west was my father, and there they were, far
away but always with me. I vowed to reach out and tell them how much
they mean to me. We'd lived in different provinces for fifteen years, and
I had to do better to show my gratitude for the life they gave me.

As profound as a beach walk can be, mine wore a deep groove in my
memory, vivid as any milestone moment I'd had before.

Now, the one flaw in my "set" and "setting" arrangement was the
absolute necessity of leaving my safe beach and lugging my gear into the
pitch-dark forest, where my deluxe hanging palace awaited. I steeled
myself, flipped on my headlamp, and plunged in. A snapping sound
froze me solid.

"Hello?" I said. No answer. Just a, a, raccoon? Some kind of animal,
but definitely a small one. I scanned the area with my light and the old
man's beard was alive, oozing a lustrous, putrid green. I shuddered.

"Okay man, you got this." I had to power through the perceived
horror movie landscape and just get my ass in that hammock. When I
did, an actual owl threw out three shockingly loud hoots.

"Breathe man," I whispered. It was a battle now. Me versus my senses.

Somehow, after many rounds of deep breathing, I managed to part
ways with my waking mind, and I remember seeing it slide away ghost-
swift, and it was waving at me. Then, as my doors clicked shut, only
nothingness remained, and I was gone.

Chapter 7

BYGONE DAYS

Many people think a ghost can speak only if
the human opens the conversation.
—— *Bluenose Ghosts*

My mind was clear and my heart light as I coaxed the Ox over a last hump in the faded asphalt road and pointed his horns at the yellow house marking the T-stop junction of the riverside village of Port Clyde. From Sandy's description, I recognized the arched green iron bridge across the mouth of the shimmering Clyde River and veered right, coming to a halt beneath a venerable oak tree.

Frantic sounds came from the water as a congregation of ducks relocated. I guessed from the high sun that it was somewhere in the mythical realm of lunchtime.

"Eleven-eleven, make a wish," I heard as the door opened and Flint the duck toller wiggled my way. Sharon stood in the threshold, a brown-haired woman with a big smile on her face.

"I was pretty sure you wouldn't be comin' by," she said, "but Sandy knew ya would. C'mon in."

"There y'are," said Sandy. "You survived the night I see."

"Yep, slept pretty well, finally."

"Well," Sharon said, "you make yourself at home. Sandy's excited to talk sailing with ya."

After removing my dusty shoes and receiving another wet kiss from Flint, I followed Sandy into the carpeted living room and sunk into a wooden rocking chair with a pillow-from-heaven on it. Sandy sat down gingerly on a loveseat, and I noted his beige-on-beige wardrobe.

Sharon had joked the night before that Sandy only wore beige, and, "He even had to have a beige truck!"

Sandy had smiled, his kind eyes crinkling behind his glasses. "Gotta be one with nature, right?"

Sunlight flooded the cozy living room, and I craned my neck to take in the bird-themed artwork and family photos, one of which had five high school graduation portraits grouped together, three girls and two boys.

"Those are my kids," Sandy said, following my eyes.

"I've got three daughters myself," Sharon chimed in, handing me a cup of coffee as she walked back to the kitchen.

"Beautiful home," I said.

"Yes, thank you," Sandy said. "I love sittin' here and watchin' the birds on the river."

I basked in the warm Nova Scotian hospitality as Sandy told me about his career in fisheries conservation, his wild days winter camping, and his love for the area, especially the empty dog-walk beaches dotting the local harbours.

"Why don't you show him your books," Sharon called from the kitchen.

"Books?" I said, my interest piqued.

"Oh, yes," Sandy said, standing up and turning for the den. "If you're interested in sailing, you'll love these."

In my wildest Slocum dreams I couldn't have conjured a better turn of events than the antiquarian feast I was about to undertake.

Sandy returned and placed two battered tomes on the coffee table, saying, "Have a look at this one first." The broken and faded green spine and mottled brown cover spoke of the nineteenth century, and when I opened it up, more careful than a rare-books archivist, I gasped. There, in immaculate hand-inked calligraphy, was this title page: "Journal of Events 1874 by Charles W. Seeley of Barrington, NS."

"That's my great-grandfather's sailing log," said Sandy. "He was a sea captain for fifty years or so, right at the same time as Slocum."

"Wow…"

"Yep," he continued, "he kept great notes, that's for sure."

As I leafed through the brittle pages, Sandy told me all about how Charles and his two brothers, George and Henry, had worked on ships at the peak of the Age of Sail, running cargo from Nova Scotia to Calcutta and all ports in between. Charles, the savviest of the lot, had once reached Liverpool from New York by dead reckoning, having compensated for a broken sextant with only a compass, a watch, and the moon.

"He was a gifted navigator," Sandy said with pride.

"Like Slocum," I blurted out. "Slocum was a lunarian too."

"That's right," said Sandy, "gotta be a math whiz to steer by the moon, eh?"

As Sandy sat back, I lost myself in the pages of lilting script, the ink flowing with tangible energy, and I pictured the quill in the hand of Captain Seeley, scrawling away thoughtfully in his snug cabin as his great vessel ran under full sail. *Just like Josh*, I thought.

"And see this," Sandy said, pulling me from my reverie. He pointed to an entry that told of his grandmother's birth aboard Seeley's ship as they lay at anchor in the Bay of Bengal, dated 1884 and underscored by the exact latitude and longitude.

"She was born at sea," Sandy said, sitting back. "She lived aboard until she was eight years old. I remember her telling me stories about pickin' flyin' fish off the deck and havin' 'em for lunch. She helped tend the little garden on board too."

At one point, I lifted the book to my nose and inhaled deeply, savouring the woody scent of ancient paper.

"You must be hungry," Sharon chirped.

Sandy and I cracked up.

"Really though," she said, "you boys ready for a bite? Sandy's still a kid—he likes peanut butter sandwiches with milk."

"Perfect," I said, my stomach lurching to life. "I'd love a sandwich. Thank you so much."

Before moving on to the second book, Sandy flipped to the final pages of the first one and showed me how Charles had run out of room and just kept on writing, his notes criss-crossing earlier entries at a forty-five-degree angle, just barely decipherable. I smiled as I pondered my own desperate notebook scribbles, words doubling up as the blank pages dwindled.

"And he had a sense of humour too. Look here," Sandy said, running his finger along a sequence of windswept cursive. "It says, 'Hasn't been enough wind in 24 days to blow the stink off a man.'"

We had a good laugh at that one.

I tried my best not to inhale my PB-soaked white bread as Sandy regaled me with stories of Port Clyde's shipbuilding past, when there was not one but five bustling shipyards up and down the local harbour.

Then we turned to the other, equally battered book. It was bound by two rusty screws in the short edge spine, giving the marbled brown cover the aspect of a vintage stenographer's pad. In faded gold-leaf font, the cover read "The Ghosts of Bygone Days."

Ghosts? A jolt of excitement shot through me.

I could tell Sandy was pleased with my giddiness. He built suspense by placing his hand slowly on the cover, saying, "Now Ryan, this is my great-uncle George's work. He was the artist of the family, and he took it upon himself to type up Charles's notes on every single American and British square rigger, bark, and schooner he'd known in his fifty years at sea."

As he lifted the thick cover open, I saw a much different sight than Captain Seeley's wall-to-wall handwriting. This was a list, neatly laid out in three typewritten columns per page, of capitalized ship names, illuminated by spectacular watercolours with quirky captions. Sandy pointed to one, a three-master with dozens of square sails faded blue on a watercolour sea, with the words "Coming home with the tea: Clipper ship *Ariel*, 858 tons. London to Hong Kong 80 days, Foo Chow to London 78 days."

"Incredible," I said, "this would have taken years to make."

"Yes," Sandy said, speaking on the inhale in classic Nova Scotian fashion. "Labour of love, this one."

The next half-hour passed in a blur. Once I realized I might be able to find direct evidence of Joshua Slocum himself, I set to my task with zeal, searching for and finding typed entries for the *Aquidneck*, Slocum's 138-foot bark, and the *Northern Light*, the 220-foot clipper ship that Slocum was the thirty-seven-year-old captain and part owner of.

On a later list, I pointed out to Sandy that the *Northern Light* had run from San Francisco to Boston in seventy-eight days, presumably around treacherous Cape Horn at the southern tip of South America. It blew my mind to learn that a feat like that was a commonplace occurrence at the zenith of the Age of Sail.

"I can't imagine what it would have been like to be a captain," I mused.

"Yass," Sandy said, "ya gotta be the toughest man on the crew, gotta be tougher than them. Crew members weren't the finest of society."

Being the sailing kook that I am, I let the floodgates open on my curiosity. Sandy was game, teaching me what "belay" means, "clawing off a lee shore," what "barques" and "gaff rigs" and "bulwarks" are, the works.

I sat leaning so far forward on my rocking chair that I nearly spilled out. At one point, he showed me a drawing by his great-uncle of a massive schooner running full tilt in an invisible wind.

"Imagine," Sandy said, catching my glance, "climbing up that rigging in a gale."

"What do you mean?" I shot back. "Like, actually climb way up there?"

"Yass, y'had to. No safety ropes either, just up there flyin' in the breeze. Unfurl, change sails, take 'em up, put 'em down, shake 'em out, or take 'em in."

"Crazy," I whispered, adrenalin coursing through me. I've always loved climbing and there's no tree I won't scale, but those towering masts attached to a lurching, fast-moving wooden boat? It looked like pure madness to me.

After catching my breath, I brought our conversation back to Slocum, the only sailing subject I knew a few things about. Sandy was keen, so

I told him how Slocum's career went downhill when he hit forty, when he sold his share in the *Northern Light*; how the Age of Steam rendered his sailing mastery obsolete; how he had to watch as the *Northern Light* and many other magnificent sailing vessels had their masts chopped off to become steamships, or worse, coal barges towed behind steamers. By the time Slocum turned fifty, he was broke and looking for work on the Boston docks. If it hadn't been for the fateful gift of a free, albeit derelict, oyster sloop, Slocum would have been sunk.

"The SS *Dewart Castle*, my grandfather's last vessel," Sandy followed, "was converted to steam. Lots of fine sailboats were. Shame that."

He exhaled a wistful sigh. "Yessir, I can't sail anymore. I had five boats in the past, but I sold the last one back in 2013. I'm seventy-three now. I've had four operations on this knee in the past two years, ended up with infection in the bone. Got a foot and a half of steel in my leg now. Mobility's really restricted. I couldn't bounce around on the deck of a boat anymore."

Sharon popped in and brought the levity back. "Ya," she joked, "he convinced me to retire right before his operations, so I looked after him for the past two years...some retirement, eh?"

"How long have you two been together?" I asked.

"Well," Sharon replied, "I lost my husband back in 2009, so we've been together...what, Sandy, since 2013 or so?"

"We get along real well," Sandy said.

"He's a pretty persuasive talker!" Sharon joked. "I like to say I went from the administrator of a long-term care facility to the owner of a woodshed."

That brought the biggest laugh yet, Sandy leading the charge. When it subsided, he took a deep breath and looked toward the photos of his kids. Sharon and I followed his gaze.

"She's an angel," he said, nodding at Sharon. "She's got wings on her back. We were just startin' to see each other—we were gettin' pretty thick really—but when my son, Richard, was killed...if she hadn't of been here, I don't think I woulda survived it."

Sharon put her hand on Sandy's knee.

"She's my angel," Sandy repeated.

The mood somehow elevated from there, and soon I found myself outside posing for a picture with Sandy, the Ox resting steadfast in front of us.

"Say cheese," Sharon said. "Can I text this to your wife?"

"Please do," I said, "and if you don't mind, let her and the girls know I'm safe, happy, and healthy."

"Will do," Sharon said, "and oh ya, she texted me this morning and asked me to tell ya that there'll be a surprise package waiting for you at the Tusket Falls Brewery."

"The brewery?" Sandy piped in. "Now that's a life partner right there!"

"She knows me," I laughed.

Once I'd stashed the cookies and banana Sharon generously supplied, I showed my gratitude by squeezing my muted horn as loud as I could and rolled away across the green bridge. When I ventured a look back, Sharon and Sandy were still standing in their driveway, side by side.

Last night as we were sailing, we were off shore a ways,
I never will forget it in all my mortal days,
It was in the grand dog watches I felt a thrilling dread,
Come over me as if I heard one calling from the dead.

Right over our rail there clambered all silent one by one
A dozen dripping sailors, just wait till I am done,
Their faces were pale and sea wan, shone through the ghostly night,
Each fellow took his station as if he had a right.

They moved about before us till land was most in sight,
Or rather I should say so, the lighthouse shone its light,
And then those ghostly sailors moved to the rail again,
And vanished in an instant before the sons of men.

These verses, sung by Mr. Gordon Young of Devils Island, were recorded by Helen Creighton in 1928. It's one of dozens of such tales found in chapter 6 of *Bluenose Ghosts*, aptly titled "Phantom Ships and Sea Mysteries."

Drowned men returning, wrecked ships appearing in the fog, brushes with "hot breath" spirits in the cabin, sudden visions that convince family members ashore that a disaster has befallen their loved one, steady shrill noises that only cease when a body is found, cursed ships no captain will set foot on — these and many more tales from the lips of Scotian sea dogs convince a reader that, yes indeed, folks up and down the shore have had ample run-ins with seabound spirits.

Helen Creighton must have been a magical listener, because stories poured out in her presence. She was a good conduit; she honoured the storyteller's truth. "Such strange things happen sometimes," she wrote. "To the skeptical they are no more than coincidence." She knew deep down that things happened outside of her consciousness that could not be explained away.

And she had that quality all great teachers have: she was a conversation catalyst, not a dominator. "Wise men do not tempt the fates as you will see by the testimony of a man from Seabright," she writes, before giving centre stage to the willing speaker.

Among the many sea mysteries she collected, one stands out for its miraculous outcome. Rather than being haunted by a spirit, the lucky shipwrecked sailors were rescued by one. Creighton kicks it off in her signature style, writing, "Well, here is the story of a dream, told to me in the 1930s by Captain Joe Boyd of Yarmouth, a man many of my readers will remember."

The tale involves two brothers, one a captain, and the other a first mate, bound for New York from London on a clipper ship. They'd been under lowered topsails for nearly a week, running through a heavy gale that stirred up treacherous seas. At breakfast one morning the captain tells his brother of a dream he had about a crew of sailors lashed to the deck of a different boat, their hands held out to him. The first mate remarks that his brother "was a quiet chap and not given to any funny stories," so, after being pestered by the dream all day, he climbed up in the mizzen rigging, and scanned the stormy water. That's when he saw the wreck.

"We changed our course," the first mate says, "and when we reached the wreck we found sixteen men in the last stages of exhaustion lashed to the rigging." The rescued sailors later claimed that they had prayed for help, their hands extended in the exact way described in the captain's dream.

"Make The Hawk Before Dawk!" That's what I whisper-yelled after a thorough inspection of my latest ripped-out backcountry map. There was Baccaro Point and Cape Sable Island dipping their granite toes in the vast Atlantic, both spots hanging like jewels off the blacktop necklace that is Highway 103. I committed to circumnavigating both, and, hopefully, squatting in the best-named town in the province, The Hawk.

Baccaro Point's claim to fame is its status as the southernmost point on the Nova Scotian mainland, but Cape Sable has the trump card: it actually *is* the province's southernmost point. Both fingers of land are surrounded by water and blessed with long sandy beaches, and they are forever bonded by the twin twinkling lighthouses that have blazed fishermen their bearings for generations.

Rolling away from Port Clyde in a fresh crosswind, the Ox and I tacked our way south on the white line of Port La Tour Road. The landscape morphed from deciduous forest to wetland, and I was welcomed by a smattering of redwing blackbirds, diving from bulrush to bulrush. The clean air was so oxygenated that when I drew huge breaths, I got dizzy and had to pull over.

A road sign told me I was in Cape Negro, but I thought it had to be some kind of prop from a movie set. Cape Negro? Seriously?

Yes, the place had that unfortunate name, and I thought back to Jessie and Sherry at the Black Loyalist Heritage Centre, and how hard they must have rolled their eyes when they saw Cape Negro still on the map, even after the municipality of Barrington had voted unanimously to ask the Nova Scotian government to speed up the name-changing process. Jessie and Sherry would know the name dates back to Samuel de Champlain, who decided in 1604 that Cape Negro would be a solid choice. And I'm sure, like me, they would see a name alteration as essential and not history-erasing.

More tranquil scrubland carried me to the dead-end Baccaro Point loop, where I was promptly and good naturedly heckled by a local riding a mountain bike that sounded more like a lawn mower.

"Ya need an engine on dat ting!" he yelled as we passed each other. He was wearing suspenders over a yellow plaid shirt, a pair of battered aviator glasses, and one of those helmets that looks like a Styrofoam cooler.

"I agree!" I called back.

The motor-assist motif persisted as I approached the treeless expanse of the point in a wicked headwind, pumping my knees in futility as I was passed by a cute couple in matching orange construction-style vests riding e-bikes, their pedal speed curiously at odds with the elements. When we chatted over snacks at a picnic table in the lee of the candy-striped lighthouse, they told me how their horizons had been opened by their e-bikes, how they were getting more exercise now than ever, and how I was crazy not to have one on my bike, especially considering the bulk I was carrying. We all looked at the Ox, and they were absolutely right: it looked like Santa's sleigh.

"Mine's a *knee*-bike," I dad-joked.

I made a prideful vow that I would resist the raging e-bike craze as long as I could. Then I added two more notches to my handlebar tally now totalling nine outright mentions that the Ox would be better if electrified.

Three hours of wind and sun later, I dragged my scorched carcass across the bridge marking Barrington Head. The thickening traffic surprised me, and I took to the gravel shoulder until I reached the merciful sidewalk of busy Barrington Passage. Sobeys, Pizza Delight, Wilson's Home Hardware, Nickerson's No Frills, even McDonald's, these I pedalled by in a daze, unaccustomed to the commercial world I'd left behind in Shelburne. Clearly this spot—and the arrow-straight causeway connecting Cape Sable Island to the main — was the shopping nexus of the area.

As I was now weak with hunger, I made for the most locally owned restaurant I could find, the excellent JB's Steak and Seafood. Then I did what any upstanding non-e-biker would do: go all in on the twenty-four-dollar creamed lobster dinner. No regrets there, aside from the sacrificed hour of fading daylight that rendered my *Make The Hawk Before Dawk* proclamation only achievable by headlamp.

An imminent sunset lit my dicey path across the busy causeway to an even busier Cape Sable Island, where I was about to follow a tip from a waitress who had clearly never tried to set up a hammock tent before.

Truck after truck, every third one exuding the skunkiest of weed smoke, tore by me as I held my arms rigid, my whole mindset intent on survival. I will admit, at that moment, to the generation of a spiteful theory I thought might explain what I was witnessing. Here it is: the size of a Cape Sable Islander's testicles is inversely related to the enhanced clearance, extra-large tires, and apocalyptically loud exhaust of his truck. Mean-spirited thinking from a holier-than-thou cycling purist, right? Right. But at that moment it felt to me like these monster-truck man-children were out to crush me. I needed rest, and soon.

When I rolled into the parking lot behind Stoney Island Beach, I bit my lip in disappointment. Treeless dunes, beautiful treeless dunes. After poking around in the dusk and trying on a few desperate tarp-camping scenarios, I started back up the hill and was stunned to see a pair of live oxen trotting my way. A red wooden yoke held the horned beasts shoulder to shoulder, their stoic white faces bedazzled by a V-shaped brocade that immediately made me think of Crystal the Feral Chocolates mystic. As they lumbered by, bells clanking, a waft of livestock musk drifted over me. I nodded to the man who was guiding them, and he tipped his straw hat. I looked around, as if to make sure someone else was seeing what I was seeing.

"Your brethren," I said to my Ox, patting his cold black steel frame.

In near-pitch darkness, I made the desperate call to sleep behind a church just off the main road. I parked the Ox parallel to the vinyl-clad wall and pegged the tarp on an angle, propping the Tombstone as a kind of barricade at the opening by my feet. I knew I was exposed, but I didn't care. Once I got snug, a spotlight came on and bathed me in light, but this time I just pulled my toque over my eyes and twisted my earplugs home, muffling in vain the guttural snorts of each enhanced exhaust system that passed by.

The only thing between me and the next day was a terrifying dream. In it, a woman dressed in white approached me and put her arm around my shoulder, tightening her grip until I realized she was trying to choke me out. I woke up gasping for breath, both nostrils stuffed shut by the moisture-laden air. For the rest of the night I breathed through my mouth, my snores harmonizing with the howls of a nearby coyote.

If wisdom's what you're after, take a table at the Barrington Passage McDonald's on a weekday morning. That's where I found myself after a dawn-patrol circumnavigation of Cape Sable Island, a run blessed by a seagull-crowded sunrise over The Hawk's superb silver sand beach.

With my Egg McMuffin devoured, I set to scrawling in my notebook, furiously trying to capture the conversations between the animated octogenarians around me. Here's a sampling of what I caught:

"I'm puttin' my wood in a shed where the wind blows through it, dries real good."

"Black floys? Yep, moskitas still some bad too."

"Wassisname doyed, wife was Trudy."

"Good mornin' trouble."

"Right straight."

"One of them alkaline rivers, de red ones?"

"None of these politicians figured it out yet, but our system could be fixed in two days."

"Minimum wage? Should be a maximum wage!"

"Most every time I gotta sneeze three times, don't know what causes it."

And my personal favourite:

"Five dollars for Ronald McDonald socks? I'd look right sexy in dem!"

When the crowded booth of six older fellas in hats emptied out, it was filled immediately by six elderly ladies clutching purses. Jokes and joviality seasoned the air, an undercurrent of laughter leaving no room for the laptop-induced silence of the cafés back in Halifax. Even the employees got the memo. One younger woman with her shiny red McDonald's visor pulled low bounced from booth to booth, cracking good-natured jokes and smiling wide. It was a true South Shore happening, and it made my sketchy visit to Cape Sable worth it.

Here was an obvious key to life, offered to me on a fast-food tray and echoed by Sharon and Sandy the day before: friendship, laughter, kindness, lightness of spirit. In the face of a sombre and cynical world, sometimes the best and only thing to do is have a good laugh. I'd been taking my exploration of death and the spirit world quite seriously, I knew, hoping that my sober approach might grant me access somehow. But there, in the Barrington Passage McD's, I saw folks at the tail end of their lives having an absolute time, scoffing in the face of destruction.

Was Slocum like that too? I wondered. All the pictures I'd seen of him showed a straight, piercing gaze. Was I chasing a dark spirit?

As I took a sip of coffee and looked up from my notebook, a bald man with a lazy left eye shouted at me, "S'dat yer bike, young fella?"

We all looked through the window at the Ox, standing stock still on his kickstand.

"Oh," I stammered, "uh, yes. Yes it is. I'm heading to Brier Island...hopefully."

"Pretty hilly down dere," he chuckled. "Hope dat ting's got electric assist!"

Chapter 8

HALF-BAKED

The supernatural in Nova Scotia is not a subject talked about
for the sole purpose of entertainment. For many of us,
it is part of our way of life.
——*Bluenose Ghosts*

My knees popped in unison as I folded my wrecked body into the weathered picnic table. Spread before me was a feast fit for a dirtbag prince: freshly filled water bottle, ice-cold can of Coke, plastic knife and fork, tiny packets of salt and pepper, industrial-strength napkin, and the centrepiece, a piping-hot circular throwaway tinfoil pan topped with a disk of white cardboard.

As I carefully worked the aluminum rim and eased off the topper, a heavenly aroma slammed my olfactory receptors. Part spiced chicken and part rich creamy potato, the plain greyish-white delicacy described by Yarmouth-area author Sandra Phinney as "the ugliest, best tasting food in the world" smelled of one thing in its totality: the spirit of Acadie. This was my first tryst with a true Acadian-made rappie pie, and I intended to make it count.

For rappie rookies like myself, there is much to learn about what many Acadian Nova Scotians consider the epitome of comfort food.

Most food scholars agree that the dish traces back to the late eighteenth century, when Acadian families returned to Nova Scotia after being cruelly turfed out by the diabolical British in what's known as Le Grand Dérangement—the Great Deportation—which spanned the years 1755–1763. Over that time, more than ten thousand Acadians, many of whom traced their ancestry on the land back multiple generations, were forcibly loaded on ships and sent sailing for France and the fledgling New England states.

Why? It's complicated, but the British knew the Acadian land was the most fertile, and they also wanted to "cleanse" the region of French culture, so they enacted a policy that inadvertently led to the invention of the rappie pie.

Most of the exiled Acadians were anxious to reunite with family and friends on their ancestral land, so when the British lifted the deportation order in 1763, a steady trickle of returnees became a stream. Did they get their mature farmland back? Of course not. As soon as they left, the British government summoned as many New England Planters as they could and handed the heartland to them. That's why, in 1767, a crew of hardy and hungry Acadians showed up in the rugged Pubnico region and set to work growing whatever they could, namely potatoes, the only crop that seemed to thrive in the thin, hardscrabble soil. A new Acadian culinary culture was born.

The traditional rappie pie consisted of twenty pounds of potatoes and could feed a family of fifteen. Making the "queen bee of casseroles" took all day, and everyone pitched in, grating the potatoes and squeezing out the starchy liquid with cheesecloth. The genius stroke, a creative Acadian twist, was replacing the potato liquid with steaming-hot stock created by whatever meat was handy, be it fowl, beef, pork, rabbit, or even fish. Once the supercharged potato mixture was loaded with chunks of meat, it was baked for as long as it took to get golden brown on top. The resulting gelatinous filling is an acquired texture, challenging to the outsider but revered by those who grew up digging into it. No wonder this communal meal evokes such strong feelings in the hearts of Acadian descendants today.

My steaming rappie had its own story of communal kindness and dubious transportation. When I bought it at D'Eon's Rappie Pie, a lively micro factory in West Pubnico, I asked the white-aproned lady if I could eat it cold, and her grimace told me I'd have to find an oven somehow. *Improbable*, I thought, but I forked over my five dollars for the pie anyway.

Dry bag and panniers full, I knew the rappie's only option was to ride open-air, come what may. I arranged two bungees — one holding it down, the other providing a backstop — and strapped it upright on the Tombstone. After a few bumpy kilometres, I knew my rappie was secure.

Many road hours later, I found myself in the office of the near-empty Castle Lake Campground, between Wedgeport and Yarmouth, excitedly booking a secure camp spot for the night. On impulse, I released my rappie and brought it with me to the counter.

"What's that y'got there?" said Sheila, the campground manager. She had the welcoming air of a genuine South Shore local.

"That's my rappie pie," I said, patting it awkwardly.

"Not plannin' to eat it cold, are ya?"

"Well, I actually am. I've been biking for six hours, and I could eat raw horsemeat I'm so hungry."

"Nope."

"Nope?"

"Not on my watch yer not. Give it here."

For a hot minute, I thought she wanted to steal my rappie, but then I noticed the full kitchen behind her. So I slid my baby over.

"I'll heat it up for ya," she said. "If this is your first rappie pie, it'd be a sin not to do it right. You go find yourself a campsite, get freshened up, and come back in an hour."

"Thank you so much," I almost yelled.

"Not a problem," she said. "Gotta feed the hungry."

And did I ever make that sunset hour count. After choosing a secluded spot in the woods, I stripped the Ox, strung up the hammock, grabbed my pile of filthy rags and speed walked to the laundry room, where I washed my clothes for the only time in three-plus weeks. Once

I'd slid my loonie home and started the washer, I raced over to the shower building and stood beneath a scalding torrent of water for ten straight minutes. Just before I fetched my rappie, I switched my clothes to the dryer and stood there, feeling fresh and famished in equal measure.

"You're in for a treat," said Sheila, as I opened the office door and stepped into a warm waft of Sunday supper scent.

"Now look," she said, suddenly serious, "you have to do this right. Here's cutlery, salt and pepper—don't be shy—and butter."

She pointed to two full paper cups stuffed with yellow gold.

"Y'let that melt on top, eh? That's the key."

"All of it?" I asked, wondering if the sheer volume of butter would send me into cardiac arrest.

"Yass! All of it! And you'll need a Coke to wash it down."

After wrapping it all up in a plastic bag, she handed it over and said, "There ya go, the only way to eat rappie pie."

"Thank you, Sheila," I said, taking my treasure. "You are my queen."

"You bet I am," she fired back. "Enjoy!"

Back at my picnic table, I plunged the plastic fork into my well-buttered rappie and promptly burned the roof of my mouth, chewing wide open as if my throat was a raging inferno. The hot gooey mixture of shredded chicken and gelatinous filling lit up my taste buds, and I set to gorging as only a lonely, hungry man in the woods can do. Nothing pretty about it. Though I'm devoid of Acadian heritage, in that moment I felt blissfully French.

The stretch of Highway 103 from Barrington to the city of Yarmouth is an uninspiring run of blacktop pushing northwest through mostly scrub forest. It's an excellent choice if efficiency is the goal: forty-three minutes is all it takes. Day and night it pulses with vehicles, all roaring from Point A to Point B. If a driver never left the highway, they'd have no idea they were missing a unique, island-studded, wetland-drenched expanse of ragged land, where warm-hearted locals live modest lives and speak in a French brogue that would make any anglo head spin.

The same stretch took me a full four days to cover. Slow and loopy never wins the race, but it sure does allow the raw beauty of "Sou'west Nova" to show itself, to breathe.

The days and nights of open exposure were adding up, and I set Yarmouth in my mind as a beacon of leisure, the break I would need as I sleuthed for Slocum on the streets he walked back in 1895. There he made his final tweaks to the *Spray* before leaving North American soil behind for over a thousand days. He knew a recharge was necessary to prepare for the myriad challenges of a solo Atlantic crossing; I felt it might be wise to follow suit.

The Yarmouth area was also home to the Redneck Psychic, a shadowy medium I'd been hearing rumours about. Two separate people had mentioned her. The name intrigued me, that's for sure. If I couldn't commune with the ghost of Joshua Slocum in my own way, maybe some professional help was in order.

Headwinds, drizzle, bugs, scorching sun — this was my new normal, and I pedalled through it all with a gritty smile on my face. It felt to me that I was a new person, a slightly unhinged one, open to any and all abnormal happenings. In retrospect, my exhausted mind had become a kind of cauldron fired not by reason but by flighty imagination. Each new experience felt like an ingredient, something tangible I could add to a metaphorical mixing bowl and whisk together. If I baked it all up, what would I have? A kind of mind gumbo. A mental meal. A one-of-a-kind Sou'west Nova psychic rappie pie.

If, for some odd reason, one were looking to achieve the same mental state, here is a list of essential vignettes from the deepest of the deep South Shore.

One Testimonial from a UFO Eyewitness

Go to the Shag Harbour Incident Interpretive Centre. Wait patiently until Laurie Wickens, a grizzled man with the thickest of all South Shore accents, arrives in his dusty pickup and lets you in for a five-dollar cash donation. Listen to his first-hand account of the events of October 4, 1967, when he saw a low-flying object crash into the harbour, float for a while, then sink. Hear how this incident was reported by eleven other

people, and how the craft, never found, was referred to as an uniden-
tified flying object in Government of Canada documents. Stare at the
pickled alien baby on the desk as Laurie asks you, "How come y'got a
black surfboard? Tryin' t'get a great white to come up'n attack ya?"
Laugh nervously.

One Animal Skull, Likely Baby Seal

Amble into the roadside spruce to relieve yourself and pick up a small,
bleached skull tinged with green lichen. Admire the wide-spaced eye
sockets and sharp incisor teeth that fall into your hands. Take the skull
back to your bicycle, stash the loose fangs for future experimentation,
and affix the skull to your front rack with black zip ties. Consider the
scene in *Hamlet* when he lifts the skull of his childhood jester and says his
famous "Alas, poor Yorick" speech, then name your new skull Derek and
speak an altered version to the crows assailing you with sharp cackles.
"Alas, poor Derek…" Laugh to yourself and look around to see if anyone's on the same wavelength. Only road, trees, sun, and irate birds. No
one is anywhere near your wavelength.

Nine Pubnicos, Mashed

Run the paperclip loop around Pubnico Harbour, swinging from helpful
tailwind to snail crawl–inducing headwind. Pretend you are a kind of
Pac-Man-on-wheels, consuming each new Pubnico town sign as you
inch by, starting with Lower East Pubnico and chomping Centre East
Pubnico, Middle East Pubnico, East Pubnico, Pubnico itself, Upper
West Pubnico, West Pubnico, Middle West Pubnico and, last but not
least, Lower West Pubnico. Convince yourself that each new Pubnico
pellet gives you energy, even though evidence points to the opposite as
true. When you get to Pubnico Point and set up your hammock tent in
a mossy hovel beneath a towering wind turbine, count and catalogue
your Pubnicos before you black out.

Three Acadian Blessings

While camped semi-legally at Pubnico Point in a light drizzle, bundle
up and smoke a pipe on the "scenic view" bench that faces an expanse

of dark green gorse and grey sea sky. Speak with three separate groups of fifty-something French ladies power walking in the mist, each one offering a broad smile, good humour, and a welcoming "Enjoy your night!" Know with certainty that folks from Pubnico are the kindest in a province full of kind people. Cough a few times when you mistakenly inhale, then curse quietly when you realize you haven't brushed your teeth before installing yourself in your hanging prison for the night. Recall the Acadian blessings instead.

One Cross-Shaped Cannabis "One Hitter" Pipe

Outside D'Eon's Rappie Pie in West Pubnico, converse with a heavily accented French man who opens his check shirt to reveal a large black cross on a chain. Stand awestruck as he proceeds to show you how, when the top is removed, the cavity becomes a receptacle for loose-leaf marijuana, and how, when lit, it can be inhaled. Laugh out loud when the wheezing man's buddy arrives in his truck and says, "Dat's a sure-fire way to mark a crucifix in yer chest hair." Realize that lighthearted blasphemy is alive and well on the Pubnico peninsula. But be advised: if offered a hit from the cross, it is recommended that a polite "No thank you" be your response.

Dash of Argyle Serendipity

Endure a vision of your bike's chain breaking while scaling a steep hill on a sparsely populated country road in Argyle. Listen to the gears grind under the strain of a mid-hill shift from seventh to lowest gear, imagining your shifter exploding under your weary legs. Picture how snookered you'd be if it happened here, in the absolute middle of nowhere. Then, as you crest the hill and find your bike still intact, notice a white garage with a sign reading *Kitchen Party Cycles* over the open door. Pull over and gush to the young mechanic, who recently moved there from Ontario, about how the first time you thought about bike mechanical disaster was right then, and how serendipitous the appearance of a bike shop was at that same moment. Accept the entrepreneur's stoke for your journey.

Half-Dozen Road Apples, Kicked

After trying the large front door of the imposing twin-steepled wooden Église Saint-Anne and finding it locked, stroll across the car-free road and start kicking apples. Kick one hard in the direction of your bicycle and watch it roll with intent over the gravel, across a patch of grass, skipping off the asphalt curb in a long arc before lodging itself firmly in the spokes of your front wheel. Continue down the road while the apple spins and spins, until it suddenly comes loose and spits directly up at your face, narrowly missing your helmet as you duck and cover.

One Genuine Jailhouse Scare

While touring Canada's oldest courthouse in Tusket, take the opportunity to descend, alone, into the warren of cramped jail cells below. Tiptoe down the dimly lit hallway and think about what it would be like to be a prisoner here, stuck in a cold box with a hard mattress and no running water. Approach a steel door with a small, crosshatched window at eye height and see what the solitary confinement cell looks like. Produce a high-pitched scream when you see a dummy sitting there in the corner, its blank eyes staring up at the ceiling. Leave in a haze of hilarious embarrassment and cherish the fresh air outside as the top-hatted tour guide guffaws at you.

Three Barely Withheld Tears over Beers

Roll up to the Tusket Falls Brewery, order a beer, and politely ask the manager if she's received a package with your name on it.

"Yep, got one just this morning. Here ya go!"

Take it and your fresh pint outside to the empty patio and sip your delicious elixir in anticipation of opening the package, which you can tell is from your long-lost life partner. Open only after the beer is drained, but be prepared for an unforeseen torrent of emotion when you read her love note and pull out two colourful drawings with the captions "Go Daddy go!" and "You Can Do It!" Show the waitress, and watch her eyes crinkle as she senses you're on the verge of man-crying. Choke the tears back in a show of foolish masculinity.

One Local Ghost Story

As you're sniffing out tales of the spirit, you're not surprised when a woman you meet outside La Shoppe à Carl in Wedgeport (you're there for your second rappie pie) tells you a doozy.

"Dis little girl drowned," you hear her say, "behind dat hill over dere. So sad. Well — no word of a lie — one night I heard a baby crying, and I came outside and I seen dat girl walking over de pond she drowned in. It's a haunted spot, take my word for it."

And you do, being well versed in the sheer strangeness of existence out there in those dark stunted old man's beard forests.

"How y'like yer Wedgeport rappie?" the woman asks.

You're careful to say, "Love it. Better than Pubnico's!"

One Spontaneous Original Song

Don't be surprised when you see Julien walk out of the woods with a guitar slung over his shoulder. He lives right there in a trailer, the stoned guardian of Wedgeport Point, and all he wants to do is play guitar and sing. Offer to freestyle a song as he strums along. Julien rips, and you're reminded that the backbone of Acadian culture is music. Music and rappie pie. Julien prompts you to riff on rappies, so you do, employing your awkward anglo tenor. Here's what spills out of you:

> *Out here on my bike*
> *Doin' just what I like*
> *Not worryin' much about time,*
> *More concerned about what might rhyme*
> *With rappie pie…*

Listen to Julien's gravelly *har har har* skip across Lobster Bay in the direction of those distant Pubnico windmills.

Unbeknownst to me, my psychic rappie pie was destined to be half-baked.

With visions of an actual bed in a real room in nearby Yarmouth dancing in my head, I steered the Ox down another dead-end road, this one running through the tiny village of Melbourne to its terminus at Pinkneys Point. I gathered from my crumpled map that it had the kind of open exposure to southwest swells that might form a long, peeling left-hand point break. Worth a look, for sure, even if it turned out to be dead flat. So much of surf exploration is "set-up" hunting, where prior experience with similar landscapes leads to a prediction a surfer will file away until the ideal swell and wind conditions align. After so many days lurking in the deep South Shore, my set-up catalogue was chock full. I hoped Pinkneys Point would be the cherry on top.

I knew I was getting out there when the road forged into an immense estuary, a saltwater marsh teeming with sparrows, blue herons, and piping plovers, all darting and soaring over a golden-hued landscape of ferns shot through with red and blue berries and flourishes of white and purple wildflowers. In the distance I could make out the gentle sloped drumlin that had to be Pinkneys Point.

This sensitive wetland was no place for a human, but here I was lumbering across on an asphalt snake, my sense of isolation deepening by the pedal stroke. When the road hit cobble beach, it hewed close to the shoreline, running under protection of the kind of beefy armour stone breakwall that is fast becoming a Nova Scotian symbol of impotence, our shield against the rising Atlantic and its consuming power. A quick look at the long sweeping headland told me that (a) I wouldn't be surfing, and (b) this spot might light up on a south swell with northeast winds. I filed the intel away and clenched my teeth for the climb into town.

Tidy bungalows on close-cropped lawns speckled the rise, topped by an expansive cemetery with a lifelike crucified Christ looming over shiny gravestones with names like Doucette, Pothier, Saulnier, Surette, and Cottreau stamped on angel-head scrolls. A cruisy downhill left me at an industrial fishing wharf festooned with lobster boats. It was clear the locals of Pinkneys Point made their living from the sea.

As I began to double back, a dipping sun meant only one thing. I'd written off the hammock back in the saltmarsh, noting the lack of trees, and now I knew that boldness would be required if shelter was to be found. I stopped at the cemetery for a Snickers and quickly hatched an ill-fated plan to sleep in the utility shed that stood open behind the field of tombstones. *It looks dry*, I thought, *and maybe the maintenance man next door would be okay to let a wayward traveller have it for the night.*

I mustered up the courage to knock on the little white house and immediately regretted it. After a storm of rabid dog barks, the front door flew open, and there stood an unshaven man in his thirties with a stained white T-shirt tucked into grey sweatpants. I flinched as the dog came flying at me, but he just sniffed me aggressively and kept going. The man glared.

All I could think to say was, "Is this your cemetery?"

As his scowl deepened, a little girl, maybe five years old, appeared beside his leg, her white dress eerily ghost-like. She scowled at me too. I took a few steps back, and after shooing the girl inside, the man slammed the door and snapped the deadbolt home.

Fair enough. Who was I to waltz up unannounced and ask for lodging? I had left my ethical moorings and was now floating around in a privacy-disturbing stew of entitlement. With no hope of home nor hammock, I had only one option left: Tarpsville.

As I fled the habitations of Pinkneys Point, I noticed a cobble ridge extending back where the road turned inland. It looked isolated, but I would need a dose of brute strength to push the loaded Ox over the backside to strike camp out of view of passersby.

After an ugly heave-fest, I chose two flat stones and levelled the Ox on his kickstand. Then I got to work tying the tarp to his frame. For anchors, I drove tent pegs into the sand and built piles of rocks around them, pulling everything taut as I imagined Slocum did on the *Spray*. When I had the Therm-a-Rest pumped and my sleeping bag out, I took a test lay down, wriggling into the exposed wedge shape, my feet pointing directly at a weathered drumlin-turned-island. *Could be worse*, I thought, smacking a mosquito. *Could always be worse.*

Since that longest of nights on the rocks of Pinkneys Point, I've learned that when I rationalize with myself about how there might be worse circumstances and how I should somehow exist in a constant state of thankfulness, I should read this as a signal of oncoming disaster.

I had covered all the safety bases — well above the high-tide line, 94 per cent certainty the Ox wouldn't fall on me while I slept, warm temperatures, and no storm on the horizon — but it wasn't my physical safety at stake. It was my sanity.

As last light brought a bright grey, almost silver horizon line, I stowed everything next to the Ox's wheels and zipped my sleeping bag all the way shut, pulling my toque down to just above my eyes. A minute after snapping on my headlamp to read my last few pages of *Bluenose Ghosts*, I heard the telltale buzz of a hungry mosquito in my right ear, followed by a slightly higher-pitched buzz in my left.

Thinking my light was drawing the bugs, I went dark and covered my eyes. The buzz persisted. *Remain calm*, I told myself, *this is just that time of day when the mosquitoes come out. They'll be gone in a bit.*

As I waited for what would never, ever come, I pulled my neck scarf up over my nose until I was mummy-wrapped. Still the surround-sound buzzing, still the rapid tapping of my hands as they cupped my cheeks in an Edvard Munch *Scream* style.

I reached for the earplugs and twisted them into little foam augers for my ear canals, easing them in until they expanded to fill the cavity. Soon I was warm, unpleasantly so, and I had the urge to expose my feet to cool myself. *Let the bugs have 'em*, I thought, *who cares about feet? Not I.* Soon my sleeping bag was a blanket, but I had to keep it tucked to my throat; any exposed skin became a magnet for the mosquitoes, who clearly had summoned their kin for the feast.

Breathing in the humid air became my next challenge, and I had no choice but to expose my nostrils to keep my brain from telling my body that it was suffocating. *Buzz, buzz, buzz*, in and out of range, left then right, earplugs be damned. Within an hour, I had lost every ounce of Zen I'd built up since leaving Cow Bay. I'd dealt with bugs many times before, but somehow I'd always found a way to sleep. That now seemed an impossibility.

As the darkness deepened, I alternated from angry tears to maniacal laughter to inches-from-the-surface sleep, a spin cycle that frayed my nerves so badly I took drastic action.

Jumping up in the pitch-black, my toque blinding me, I ripped and tore at the tarp, yanking whatever I could get my hands on, until my camp was a mangled heap of gear and rope. Still the mosquitoes swarmed, entertained by the frustrated screams of their favourite all-night buffet. And then, as if I'd somehow broken through a wall, I turned icy calm and just stood there. A mosquito landed on my nose and I let it have what it wanted. Another landed on my hand, and still I didn't move.

"You win," I said.

It might have been 3:00 or 4:00 a.m. when I entered zombie mode, I have no idea. As the bugs swarmed, I pulled on my headlamp and set to work methodically repacking the Ox, taking each fresh bite in stride until I was ready to roll. It felt like I was watching myself from above as my legs started their piston motion and the Ox resumed his languid rhythm across the steaming wetland, heading for who knows where. To this day, the insect-haunted night on Pinkneys Point stands as the very worst of my forty-four years.

No soul restoration for me. My psychic rappie pie was a complete bust, half-baked and inedible. If this was some kind of Acadian exam, I'd officially failed with flying colours.

PART THREE

SAILING ALONE AROUND THE WORLD

Chapter 9

BECALMED

The people of this coast, hardy, robust, and strong, are disposed to
compete in the world's commerce, and it is nothing against the master
mariner if the birthplace on his certificate be Nova Scotia.
— *Sailing Alone Around the World*

A sailor without wind is akin to a surfer without waves, their frowny
faces remarkably alike. Mother Nature rules both of them, and it is by
her fickle whims alone that propulsion may be achieved. In a nutshell,
she controls the stoke.

Down by the equator, between the latitudes of 5° north and 5° south,
there exists a region of predictably calm air dubbed the doldrums. It's
no coincidence that "doldrums" is used synonymously when describing a depressed person. "He's in the doldrums right now," a concerned
friend might say. Stagnation, lack of movement, loss of control, that's
the doldrums.

And, though sailors have often considered this state a curse on them
directly, it's an effect caused by the equator's proximity to the sun.
Being in constant close contact with that blazing ball, the air warms
and goes straight up rather than blowing horizontally, and the result is
pure calm. Before combustion came to the stinky rescue, this zone had

a deadly reputation for seafarers. Ships could be stranded for weeks on end, threatening food and water supplies, with scurvy, delirium, cabin fever, and starvation never far away. Getting through the doldrums was a matter of life and death.

It would be hyperbolic to compare a becalmed surfer's experience to the doomed sailor's, but have you ever spent time with a compulsive surfer who's been out of the water for a month or more? It's like watching a toddler on the verge of a tantrum. We walk around with a selfish and dark centre of gravity, prone to melancholy, and the longer it's flat the saltier we get. Scurvy of the surf soul, that's what it feels like. We can only pray to the Surf Gods for release. When a storm finally brushes by or a groundswell miraculously appears, we drop everything to get back out there. Schedules, jobs, family responsibilities be damned—we must pay tribute to the Gods. It seems like a sailor, when presented with a capful of wind, might react with similar self-centred zeal.

Conclusion? Baby needs his bottle.

The word "becalm" has two definitions, one scientific and the other psychic: "to keep motionless by lack of wind" and "to make calm, to soothe."

It was this second meaning that propelled my nearly catatonic self across the stunning ridge lands of Central Chebogue, past a few juicy surf set-ups, and along the quiet back roads onto Yarmouth's Main Street in search of a place to collapse. I didn't want a high-rise hotel or a chain motel but rather a kind of Worst Western, something budget and brimming with grit. Unfortunately, I had two forces working against me: a bum Magic 8 Ball prediction (*Outlook Not So Good*) and the recent knowledge that Yarmouth was hosting the Nova Scotia 55 Plus Games, meaning the place would be swarming with flush boomers who had likely locked down every rentable room in Sou'west Nova.

I pedalled past the imposing concrete monstrosity known as the Rodd Grand Yarmouth and the low-slung, '70s-era Best Western Mermaid Yarmouth without more than a glance.

Only if I get desperate, I thought. After that, I struck out on the YMCA Hostel (gone), a motel that had been converted to apartments (no vacancy), and a mothballed corner pub/inn that had seen better decades.

When Main Street spilled me out of the downtown into a residential area, my hope and health *Low Fuel* light came on full blast. I needed a whiff of luck to make something happen.

That's when I saw it, a green wooden sign with red trim and the words *Lakelawn Motel* emblazoned in gold. I struggled to keep the Ox upright as I scanned the scene: there before me was a nineteenth-century house with two single-storey tentacles extending out in a wide C-shape, each dotted with numbered rooms facing the central parking lot. Not only did the young German manager tell me that one room was available and all my new neighbours were 55 Plus Games participants and a sit-down continental breakfast with real coffee was included, but she also informed me that the mansion, originally built in 1836, was home to a friendly ghost, who lived in the crow's nest up a narrow, twisting stairway above the lobby.

"Yah," she added, "I know because every time I straighten the lamp up there, next day it is crooked again!"

"Heaven!" I wanted to shout. My impression was validated when I took the old-school clacking plastic key chain and opened the door to my sanctuary, my very own room with a roof and a window and a bathroom—tiny shower, yes!—and a firm, no-nonsense bed. One final burst of energy helped me lug my gear in, scatter it all around, take a long shower and eat the last of my gas-station sandwich ration before I fell, like an old-growth cedar, onto the bed, bouncing once, twice, and then settling, sprawled out on the stiff top sheet for the most becalming nap-turned-full-night-recharge of all time.

Fresh sea air and cottony clouds greeted me as I emerged from breakfast renewed, ready to explore the streets of Yarmouth on Chicken Tender, my trusty red skateboard. The bugs of Pinkneys Point had left my face a raw, meaty red, but I felt good, and I knew my day of Slocum sleuthing would be an illuminating one.

As I pumped down the smooth blacktop of Water Street past old factories and weedy parking lots, I saw an interlocking brick pathway winding along the waterfront, punctuated by quaint little pagodas housing historical signs.

As a dad-in-training, I've been more intentional about stopping to read signs like the ones Yarmouth had on offer, partly to get informed and partly to show my daughters what dads do—they read historical signs, from top to bottom, and they revel in the impatience of their children. At least that's what my dad used to do, and I remember never getting it until I actually read one myself. Now I know that historical signs are the essence of caring preservation and the key to grasping the context of the place you're in. And they teach tortured children patience.

I quickly found out that Yarmouth is home to the best historical signs in Nova Scotia. The first one I rolled up to was a feast for the hungry historian's senses. Period photographs of busy wharves with horse-drawn wagons and dozens of ships, railway stations with formally dressed folk waving hats, early motor coaches bumping down busy streets, even a sepia-tinged shot of an electric tram beside a team of oxen. Ticket stubs from the Yarmouth Steamship Company advertising "The Shortest and Most Direct Route from Nova Scotia to Boston" jostled playfully with silky smooth narrative like, "In the late 19th century, prosperous Yarmouth boasted of a modern and efficient urban transportation system featuring an electric street railway that replaced earlier horse-drawn omnibuses." A tidbit like that conjures a sense of what Yarmouth must have been like in its heyday, and a caption like this brings it all home: "In 1892, Yarmouth established the first electric street railway system in Nova Scotia." Aha, the city was once a powerhouse on the commercial landscape. If I'd skipped the sign, how would I ever learn that?

I sponged it all up for a solid hour, skating from sign to sign like a history-jazzed hummingbird. The ultimate nectar, however, was not a historical sign but a huge map, the kind that depicts a cityscape from above with its margins stuffed by stand-alone drawings of the city's most prominent buildings. The one I found, closest to the water, had "Yarmouth 1889" written in fancy font along the bottom. Knowing that Slocum sailed through in 1895, I could instantly imagine what he might have seen, heard, and even smelled as he haunted the dockyards in search of supplies.

Yarmouth was a big deal back then. A dense thicket of residential streets ran back from a waterfront bursting with wooden piers, each one propping up two- and three-storey warehouses, and the harbour traffic was heavy with steamers billowing black smoke, majestic three-masted clipper ships, and tiny sloops like Slocum's. Each factory is given its own frame and caption, from the Cordova Leather Works to the J. Phillips Candy factory to the Parker, Eakins & Co Wholesale Grocers and Export Dealers in Fish. And every one proudly belches smoke from its stand-alone stack.

Back of the sooty dockyards are the grand hotels, banks, court-houses, post office, and seminary, topped off by an immense domed extravagance called the Exhibition Building. Prominent residents have their homes shown off in frames too, like the immaculate gothic revival "residence of A.W. Eakins" and the Georgian beast "residence of E.K. Spinney." Along the top, and echoed by the town drawing, are a row of ten churches, each one a vaulted rectangular frame with a single spire. Baptist, Catholic, Methodist, take your pick: 1889-era Yarmouth had your spiritual needs covered. I knew from Slocum's tale that he would've avoided the holy houses in favour of a berth on his true deity, the great blue sea.

As I glided along on Chicken Tender, I scanned Yarmouth's skyline for traces of that heyday grandeur. A few spires still poked up in the blue, but the waterfront had lost much of its verve, resigned at the time of my visit to a single marina and a ferry terminal with no ferry, the last trip from Yarmouth to Portland, Maine, having run back in 2018.

I did stop at a fascinating remnant of those boom times, an old street-car that had been restored and turned into a food truck, but it was closed. It sat on its very own chunk of track, but it wasn't going anywhere soon. The marina showed signs of life, though, so I stepped onto the gangway and took a look.

One sailboat caught my eye. As I peeked into the open cabin, a young guy came out carrying a bag of garbage.

"Oh!" he said, taken aback.

"Hi," I said. "Don't mind me. Just admiring your sailboat."

"It's not mine," he said with a sheepish grin. "It's my parents'."

"Is she a sloop?" I asked, flexing my cribbed sailing lingo.

"Um, yep," he replied. "She's a forty-six-footer. We started in Baddeck, and we're heading to Bar Harbor tomorrow before running her back to Lake Michigan."

"Wait," I said, excited, "you mean you're crossing the Gulf of Maine tomorrow? Like, sailing across it?"

He looked at me quizzically. "That's right."

"Wow!"

I couldn't fathom how it might be possible to go so far in one day under wind power alone.

"Does she have a motor?" I asked.

"Um, yes, yes she does. If there's no wind we can still motor along."

"Oh, I see."

The poor guy must have thought I'd lost my marbles. He played "humour the landlubber" well though. After teaching me a few more things, he made his way to the dumpster and chucked the bag in, the lid slamming closed behind him. It sounded like a gunshot.

I strolled to the end of the pier and scratched my head. How did Joshua Slocum do it without a motor? Especially in a busy port like 1895 Yarmouth? I recalled a grainy photo of Slocum on the *Spray* with a long pole in his hands, spearing it into the water at a steep angle. That was his answer. He was all elbow grease and ingenuity.

Before I left the docks in search of the Yarmouth County Museum & Archives, I let go of a faint hope I'd been nurturing since way back in Chester. I wouldn't be sailing on this expedition. It just wasn't in the cards. Aside from the three sailboats in Yarmouth, I'd seen nothing but industrial wharves stuffed with wide-bodied lobster boats, their gurgling engines drowning out what I imagined would be the blissful near-silence of a sailboat urged on by the wind. I would have to wait until the following summer, when I might join a "learn to sail" summer camp. I pictured myself surrounded by ten-year-olds in little laser boats, ripping past me as I fumbled with the lines. Oh well, not meant to be.

I'd have to be content to see Slocum's world through his book and my imagination only.

Mildly dejected, I trudged up Forest Street, across Main, and into Yarmouth's historic residential district, where I promptly found another sign inviting me to take a Heritage Walking Tour. This sent me bouncing from one wealthy sea captain's home to the next. Towering ash and oak trees shaded the quiet streets as I stood in front of each dwelling, soaking in the detailed trim around the windows, the ornate woodworking on every beam, and the curious crow's nests topping each roof. *Folks put real energy into keeping these up*, I thought. It must be a true labour of love saving these audacious mansions from rotting into the earth.

The Yarmouth County Museum beckoned from inside the granite walls of the former Tabernacle Congregational Church, built three years after the map's record I'd been admiring back on Water Street. The vaulted space was dominated by what looked to be a thick glass space shuttle, refracting light in all directions. This was the original second order Fresnel lens used at Cape Forchu lighthouse until 1840, brought here as centrepiece for the many models of ships in glass cases that crowded the floor.

My entrance paid, the keen museum curator took my Slocum stoke in stride, pointing me to a small glass box in the corner beneath a row of sailing flags. There I found an essential clue to unravelling the mystery of Joshua Slocum. It was a scale model of the *Spray*. I swivelled my head in excitement, looking for anyone to share my joy with. Anyone? A scale model of one of the world's most famous sailing vessels, and I had to geek out alone. So be it. In an instant my respect for Slocum deepened, knowing that he was given the dilapidated *Spray* for free and that, when he first saw her up on blocks in a Fairhaven, Massachusetts, field, he knew what she was capable of if enough time and energy were spent to make her seaworthy. To be fair, Slocum was desperate back then, closing in on broke and with no prospect of seaborne employment around the bend. He was almost fifty, as well, and his second marriage was loveless. So he went all in, spending his last $553.46 and taking thirteen months to completely rebuild the *Spray*, deflecting the daily ribbing from grizzled whaling captains who kept asking, "But will it pay?" to which he responded, without fail, "I'll make it pay." Having built and rebuilt ships in his past, he had ample ingenuity, not to mention the tenacity of a wolverine. When it came time to launch his new boat, he claimed it "sat on the water like a swan." His unthinkable dream of circumnavigating alone was now an active plan.

As I circled the model, I struggled to put names to what I saw. It had a long "bowsprit," that I knew, and three taut white sails, but I couldn't recall their names. Mainsail? Jib? Gaff sail? I made out his tiny tender upturned on deck, a New England dory he'd sawn in half and which almost drowned him when it overturned off the coast of Argentina. And there was the hatch to his cabin below, which he stocked with books like Darwin's *The Descent of Man*, Twain's *Life on the Mississippi*, a full set of Shakespeare, and — my personal favourite — Cervantes's *Don Quixote*.

I leaned close to see the exposed steering wheel at the stern with a tiny version of the block-and-tackle invention he cooked up to give the *Spray* self-steering capability, carving him ample time to read every book in his library twice. Finally, I stood behind the model and admired her flared out, ultra-buoyant line, built for floating, not speed. At thirty-six feet, it was hard to imagine the *Spray* bounding up and over forty-foot rollers in the maelstrom of a Roaring Forties swell, but Slocum had faith. Faith, plus a lifetime of experience in every corner of the world's oceans, albeit on ships much bigger than the *Spray*. But I sensed the magic; the little ship exuded confidence. I shivered when I remembered that, a decade after getting back from his epic voyage, Slocum and the *Spray* finally gave up the ghost together, vanishing somewhere in the warm, shark-infested Caribbean Sea.

It was hard to move on from the perfect model and all it evoked in my fiery imagination, but I had a whole museum to see. I roamed around still preoccupied with Slocum, and I was on the verge of leaving when I came across a small room dedicated to — wait for it — oxen in Nova Scotia.

To every teenager in every class I'd ever taught, this exhibit would be the embodiment of paint-drying boredom. As a seasoned chaperone, I knew a field trip to the fascinatingly dry Yarmouth County Museum would be more about crowd control than learning. Where were those teens, though? Back in Halifax, in class with someone else. I could quietly inspect the wall display of glossy red wooden yokes, thick leather head pads, coiled reins, and heavy golden bells in blissful peace.

Before my South Shore journey, my oxen knowledge extended as far as the cheerful Maud Lewis paintings I'd seen in the Art Gallery of Nova Scotia. The display taught me that oxen were central to the settlement of Nova Scotia, and that French immigrants brought the first beasts to L'Acadie in 1610. Naming my cargo bike the Ox was apt considering the load I lugged.

"What is an Ox?" I read. "An ox is a domestic steer, a castrated bull. Castration is necessary so that the animal is less temperamental. The steer must then be trained to work before it is considered an ox." *Interesting,* I thought, *this is likely the only snippet of information teenagers would be fascinated by.*

Surrounding the artifacts were a dozen framed black-and-white photos of oxen doing their thing: in double yoke harness pulling a lobster boat; in single yoke harness next to a smiling man brandishing a whip; standing at rest with their shiny head pads, long upturned horns, and dangling bells. In every shot, there is a deep sense of resignation in the ox's stare. *I'll do this, fine,* they seem to say, *but I'm not going to get excited about it.* Before machines—and even a long time after combustion took over—oxen were indispensable members of the family, and though they were worked hard, they were treated with love and respect, given names and pride of place in the barn.

One nugget of South Shore oxen lore hit me like a bolt of lightning, sending me serious Slocum shivers. Down here, a single ox was often preferred "to pull logs through forest stands more easily than a team," and guess what a single ox was nicknamed? (Cue the teenaged glazed eyes.) A sloop! One ox, one boat, one name: a sloop. This quirky insight sent me spinning like a top right out of the museum onto the leafy sidewalk, kicking the asphalt with gusto so Chicken Tender and I could glide, glide like the wind, Slocum's aura charging us forward in search of more revelation.

Next came an epic antique shop, which I found after a half-hour rip that had more than a few locals staring at the strange interloper on wheels, my crooked sunglasses and bug-pocked face on full display. Warehouse 87 Antique Emporium opened like a secret neolithic cave, and instantly I knew it held a treasure for me. Kevin, the gruff proprietor, fielded my Slocum questions politely, steering me to the warehouse portion so I could lose myself in the crowded warren of dusty trunks, bent licence plates, old ship models, stacks of books, vintage telephones, and countless trinkets. I resisted the urge to buy a second pipe, and I could see no reason to acquire another broken timepiece, considering my rusty Westclox was still holding strong on the Ox's handlebars. I did think of Slocum's description of his Yarmouth-purchased clock, which he had to dip in boiling water frequently so it would keep ticking, how only the hour hand worked, and, incredibly, how Slocum decided to go without a sextant at all, circling the globe with only his broken clock, the moon, and the stars as guides.

I paused and inhaled the musty, dusty air I loved so much, the essence of buried time, the funk of lost eras. Aside from an intricate model of a clipper ship I coveted but knew would be the most impractical thing in the world to bring on a bike camping quest, no knick-knack told me I had to rescue it.

Just before I turned to leave, I caught sight of a red wooden object above Kevin's till, and a squint told me it was a miniature oxen yoke. My jaw dropped.

"What is it, my son?" Kevin said. "See a ghost or somethin'?" He glanced up in mock fright.

"Is that an . . . oxen yoke?"

"Yessir," he said, "that it is."

"Is it for sale?"

Kevin laughed. "Everything's for sale in here, my friend."

"Oh," I said, turning even redder, "uh . . . how much for the yoke then?"

Kevin cocked his head and inspected the dust-caked object. He scratched his chin.

"Couldn't take less than twenty-five dollars for it," he said, his eyes averted.

"Deal," I said. I was so excited that I forgot I only had twenty-two dollars in cash on me. *Oh no,* I thought, *he sounds firm.*

"Sorry Kevin," I said, "Will you take twenty-two dollars for it?"

"For sure," he said immediately, almost as if he respected me more for haggling with him.

More madman grinning as I stepped back into the glorious Yarmouth sunshine, sure in the knowledge that my acquisition was somehow cosmically essential. I looked down at the foot-long piece of carved wood, glossy red, and then it dawned on me. My miniature oxen yoke was anatomically suggestive of a two-headed phallus. I burst out laughing.

Since none of those antique clocks worked, I had to take a cue from my stomach that suppertime was approaching. I remembered seeing a sign for The Dinner Plate somewhere on Water Street, so I angled Chicken Tender in that direction and cruised in the cooling air until I saw the single-storey white stucco building with a neon red *Open* sign in the window.

The place was packed, servers flying in all directions, a lively din of conversation buzzing from the wooden booths and crowded card tables. A gregarious man showed me to the only open booth, and I watched him careen from table to table, asking how the food was and offering a kind word. I knew then that I'd stumbled on a local institution, and I made the most of it, opting for homemade fish cakes, a garden salad, and a bottle of Schooner beer. Young couples chewed and smiled at each other, older couples ate in stoic silence, whole families sat shoulder to shoulder at pulled-together tables, and a cute little baby drew the room together, his parents jostling him up and down as his grandparents looked on with pride. This was Yarmouth to me. Easy conversation, warm people, humble surroundings.

I sat back in my booth, took a sip of icy beer and soaked it all in. Just before my glorious fish cakes arrived, I noticed my paper placemat was decorated with ornate calligraphy celebrating the Chinese Zodiac, and a quick scan told me that this year was the Year of the Ox. I blinked in astonishment. It didn't matter that this was only important to people born in the year of the Ox, which I wasn't, but that, well, everything was turning up Ox. The fish cakes confirmed it: I was in the right place, doing the right thing, at the right time.

The Lakelawn Motel was lit up like a nautical lantern when I finally made it back, Chicken Tender tucked under my arm. The light with the crooked lampshade was displayed prominently in the crow's nest above the office, tilted, as the manager claimed, by a ghost. Having recovered from my scare in Liverpool, I decided to be bold and try for a closer look. The night-shift employee, a high school student tapping on her laptop, seemed keen to help.

"Any chance I might be able to see that lamp up close?" I asked.

She hesitated, but then said, "Sure, why not. I'll take you up there."

I followed her up the pocket staircase and into the room with the lamp.

"I'm told there's a ghost here," the teenager said, "but it's harmless."

"Mind if I straighten the lampshade?"

"Have at it!"

"An experiment," I said, "you know, to prove if there's a ghost here or not."

"Cool," she said, straight-faced.

On the way back to my room, I saw the Ox standing exactly where I'd left him that morning. With his burden gone and his harness off, he looked content, rested. I vowed to give him more love on the final push from Yarmouth to Brier Island. As I patted his handlebars and whispered sweet nothings in his ear, I noticed two faces staring at me from the neighbouring room. They waved at me and I waved back. What could I say? Maybe they were used to seeing people talk to their bicycles. Or maybe, like most of the people I'd crossed paths with that fine day in Yarmouth, they saw me for what I was: a beaming fool in search of a sign.

I didn't want to leave the doldrums, but I had to. Yarmouth's becalming effect was a dream, a necessary recharge to make the final push possible without losing my mind. I knew Slocum had enjoyed a few stops like these on his voyage, so I didn't feel bad. The road ahead, like Slocum's sea, looked more inviting after being away from it.

My last action, one I'd timed for my departure from the Lakelawn, was to check if the lampshade I'd straightened was altered in any way. I doubted it would be. As I fought to keep the Ox rolling, I snuck a look back and then another. Was it crooked? It looked crooked. But I was moving in the opposite direction now, away from one ghost and toward another. The lampshade was in the rear view; the spectre of Slocum rose ahead.

Chapter 10

SNUGGLERS COVE

It was an exceedingly snug nook.
— *Sailing Alone Around the World*

From April 24, 1895, to June 27, 1898, Nova Scotia–born Joshua Slocum sailed a total of 74,000 kilometres, alone at the helm of his refurbished thirty-six-foot oyster sloop, completing the first single-handed circumnavigation of the Earth. He, like the major explorers before him—Columbus, da Gama, Magellan, Drake—shifted the paradigm and opened a new perspective on the planet. After Slocum's achievement, the globe seemed smaller.

That Joshua Slocum left Boston with $1.50 in his pocket sets his achievement apart. He wasn't backed by the coffers of nations, blessed by royalty, or vetted by presidents; he did it on his own, trading goods along the way, accepting the generosity of strangers, and giving reluctant talks on his voyage to paying audiences in the ports he came to see as necessary respites from the demanding ocean. Slocum's brand of self-reliance and pluck caught the attention of a world on the cusp of a brand new century. His achievement electrified, however briefly, the modern imagination.

From the small, hanky-waving crowd on the Boston docks, he touched at Brier Island and Yarmouth before skirting up the South

147

Shore of Nova Scotia and turning east, leaving the lighthouse beams of Halifax Harbour behind.

After a stop in the Azores islands, he sailed to Gibraltar with the aim of breezing over the Mediterranean Sea through the newly built Suez Canal to the Indian Ocean. Officials in Gibraltar strongly advised against his course, citing pirates, and Slocum, being untethered to any agenda, made the quick decision to alter course and sail back across the Atlantic on a southwest tack. Throughout his odyssey, Slocum made big calls like this with a metaphorical shrug, leaning on sober reason and the advice of locals to find his line.

After inching past the Cape Verde islands in the equatorial doldrums latitudes, well supplied as he was, he rode the trade winds to Brazil and bounced down the South American coast, touching at Pernambuco, Rio de Janeiro, and Buenos Aires, where he had an emotional reunion at his first wife Virginia's grave. Then it was on to imposing Cape Horn, where, after his greatest sea adventure — more on this madness later — he emerged in a new ocean, the vast one Magellan coined Pacific.

Juan Fernández Islands off the coast of Chile came next, where Slocum sniffed around for the legend of marooned sailor Alexander Selkirk, model for Daniel Defoe's famed fictional castaway, Robinson Crusoe. Slocum then put his self-steering invention to work, locking the *Spray* on a true course and sailing an incredible seventy-three days and nights with barely a touch on the tiller, spending most of his time devouring books and writing in his cabin below.

After basking in a hero's welcome in Samoa and Fiji, he sailed through increasingly stormy waters to the coast of Australia, stopping for a quick visit in Sydney before settling in for a long season wait-out in Tasmania. There he made another whopper of a decision, forgoing the Roaring Forties run below Southern Australia for a northern skirt of the Great Barrier Reef en route to the Timor Sea and yawning Indian Ocean beyond.

At the Cocos (Keeling) Islands he swapped his cement ballast for giant conch shells, intending to sell them when he returned to the States, then continued west, sighting Madagascar but resisting his land-itch until he hit Durban on the east coast of South Africa. There he had a legendary tangle with a nineteenth-century version of the Flat Earth Society, led by a prominent head of state who disputed Slocum's assertion that, yes indeed, the world is round. Slocum's response came with a wry smile: "My voyage is proof."

Mountainous seas and fierce gales awaited him as he drove the *Spray* forward and rounded the Cape of Good Hope, a treacherous passage named to entice sailors to give it a go. Next was a long sea run to Saint Helena, where he made the mistake of bringing a hat-devouring goat on board. Then it was a return to the Brazilian coast to celebrate the crossing of his outbound line with an uncharacteristic sip of whiskey. Though he had officially now "tied the knot" on his circumnavigation, Slocum knew it wouldn't be complete until he made the States, so he sailed on, zigzagging on a northwest tack through the Caribbean and up to the mouth of New York Harbour, where the *Spray* nearly capsized in a surprise lightning squall.

At Boston Slocum basked in the fanfare of an excited crowd, but it wasn't until he eased the *Spray* back into her berth at Fairhaven and looped her lines to the "same old stake" that he could finally exhale and know, deep down, that he'd realized his vision.

No steam engine, no sextant, no safety tether to lash himself to the mast in tempestuous seas, no life buoy to speak of. This was Joshua Slocum, a bald, by then fifty-four-year-old man with nothing but a steely glare and a rock-solid respect for the object of his worship, the enigmatic sea. He hadn't shattered worlds; he was too humble to see his accomplishment that way. Instead, he'd gone out there in search of solitary adventure and found it in its purest form: good old-fashioned, high-stakes fun.

The day's first ascent almost ended mine. Here I was, entering the rolling farmland of North Chegoggin after only two days off the loaded Ox, and my burden felt impossibly heavy, as if someone snuck a lead anchor into my dry bag.

The hill rolled all right, straight up, each merciful flat followed by another mean tilt of asphalt. I hadn't seen a ridge on my map; I just knew there were a few kilometres of land between me and the Gulf of Maine, so I turned off the northbound Highway 1 and went for it. When I reached the top, I experienced the painful phenomena particular to every hill-climbing cyclist who takes a break: heaving lungs, blinking through black spots in the vision, an immediate urge to slug a full litre of water. Once I'd brought my engine out of the red, I registered a bucolic green farmland with its smattering of neat bungalows and hardwood copses, all backed by perfect-day blue and drowned in sparkling sunshine. *Hills be damned*, I thought, *this day is a blessing to cyclists, so cycle I must.*

After a stop at an antique shop, of course. This one, a peeling cedar shake barn with a slumped roofline, had a collection of ancient horse-drawn buggies on the lawn. Cliff, the proprietor's stepfather and lone clerk for the day, welcomed me into the barn and fielded my Slocum enquiries with a friendly "No idea my son, but yer welcome to have a gander."

Having struck out on my secret desire—an early edition of *Sailing Alone*—I stood outside on the gravel and shot the breeze with Cliff. In my eyes, Cliff was already a legend based on his laid-back demeanour and righteous fashion sense.

He was a heavier-set gentleman with a dark blue T-shirt pulled taut over a robust stomach and tucked into faded jeans. He had a cane in his right hand and a weathered ballcap emblazoned with *Bad Hair Day* pulled low over a set of '80s glasses that are now very much on trend. The yellow hair of his bristly moustache seemed to reach down in an attempt to merge with the grey tuft jumping out of his shirt collar. I sensed that Cliff had news for me.

"Cliff," I said, "I'm hoping you can help me out. I brought an antique with me—this wooden pole here—and I have no idea what it is. I know it's from a farm, but that's all I got."

"Lemme have a look," he said, pulling his left hand out of his pocket and extending it my way. "Hmm," he said, turning it over, "lookie here." He guided me over to one of the big wheeled buggies and held the piece out, as if matching it with something on the cart. Right behind it was a near-replica of my piece.

"Wow!" I said, "that's nuts, it's the same thing."

"It's called a singletree," Cliff said.

"A single what?"

"Singletree. It's used to steer the horse or ox. These metal bits are called trace hooks, see? The reins pull on 'em to steer."

I stood there speechless as Cliff continued, wielding his farm antique prowess in the most modest way possible. He had no idea I was stuck on just one of his words: *ox*.

"Did you say ox?"

He looked me in the eyes. "Sure, same type a thing used on d'old single ox carts too. Used to call dem sloops."

"Amazing..."

It felt like a door to a bank vault was opening in my head — a *click* here, a *whir* there — and light poured in. My singletree was from Slocum's ancestral farm, and I'd brought it here on a bicycle I'd christened the Ox for the express purpose of aiding a medium to connect with Slocum's spirit. It was too much to compute. All I could muster was another spacy "amazing." Cliff must have thought I was higher than a kite, and maybe I was.

"You okay, young fella?" he said.

I snapped back. "Yeah, I'm great. You just made my day."

"Dat's my job," he said, smiling. "Antiques change lives."

We laughed in unison.

After soaking up as much wisdom as I could, I lashed Slocum's singletree back down and readied myself for more sun-baked road. Cliff stared at the Ox, and I knew exactly what he would say before he said it.

"You gotta git a motor on dat ting, bud! I saw some guy just comin' right up dat hill the other day, guy just cruising along uphill. You gotta git one."

I smiled and nodded slowly. "You're so right, Cliff, you're so right."

With my compass pointing true north for the first time, I cruised along the winding ridge and stared at the big water that kept popping up on my left, a vast blue sheet rolling back to the western horizon line. A California sunset was on deck for later; better find a snug harbour to soak it in.

At Short Beach, the road turned inland and ran beside the apple tree–lined Darlings Lake, its sweet fragrance powering me past a string of well-kept houses, until I hit the main again, the road dubbed the Evangeline Trail. I knew I was heading back into Acadian territory, but I had no idea just how French the region stretching up St. Marys Bay would turn out to be. Was I heading into rappie pie country yet again?

Beaver River, Bartlett's Beach, Salmon River, I pedalled past them all as the sun reached its zenith and sent a quickening headwind my way. I leaned into it. The Ox felt rejuvenated and hungry for work, for blessed toil, and that's what he got, holding the white line like a champ as a cavalcade of silver-haired retirees breezed past in sensible cars. A refreshing downhill spat us out at Mavillette Beach, a known surf spot I hoped might offer up a Tombstone slide or two. Was there a wave? Nope. Though it was pancake flat, I knew exactly what all the fuss was about: "Mavs," as it's called, has to be the broadest, most walkable beach in the province. As I crossed the boardwalk over protected dunes, a runway of sand stretched off in both directions, small groups of strolling seniors dotting the low-tide landscape, dogs romping free. I found a quiet spot to eat a damp sandwich and lowered my hat to block the blaze, studying my last slice of map for a potential end game to the day.

On maps, for an incognito cycle touring grifter, a red picnic table symbol speaks of camp potential. Combine that with the forest green font of a provincial park and you're in "must scope" territory. Smugglers Cove Provincial Park fit the bill, so I circled it and vowed to reach the park before suppertime, knowing any place with that name would have to be a legitimate hideout. It even had a little Smoky the Bear–style hat next to it on the map, which, at the time, I had no idea meant Royal Canadian Mounted Police. Fortunately, my brush with the Mounties was not destined to happen that night, but later on down the road.

Aside from the stunning twin spires of the overtly French Catholic Saint-Alphonse-de-Ligouri Church, the Evangeline Trail from Mavillette to the Meteghan area was yet another collection of humble bungalows with big lawns freshened by a tangy sea breeze. I rolled on and on until the road curved toward the coast, and that's when I spotted it: a distant sliver of land on the blue horizon.

"Could it be...," I said aloud to the passing cars, grabbing brake. "Yes, it is! It has to be!"

There, past the nest of electrical wires and roadside pines, was the tip of Digby Neck I knew had to be Brier Island. My terminus, Slocum Country.

I could finally see it with my own eyes. Brier friggin' Island. There it was. Unfathomably far away, sure, but definitely there.

I cruised into Smugglers Cove as if on a cloud and ran the Ox up to a cliffside picnic table enclosure. Instantly, I knew this place would be my spot for the night. I interpreted the *No Camping* sign to mean *No Car Camping*, and I treated the *Gates Closed at Sunset* sign as insurance that, if I could stay low key until then, the whole place would be mine to respectfully squat in.

Rustling thistles fringed the picnic area overlooking a sheer granite cliff that formed one side of a horseshoe-shaped notch, its mouth pointing squarely in the direction of Brier Island, the whole of Digby Neck running in one long rising ridge to the north. For now, I was just another tourist enjoying a picturesque rest stop, so I loafed around with my arms behind my back, whistling as I went, throwing stealthy glances at the cliffside forest for the right kind of tree spacing.

"Hi there," I called out to an older gentleman in a Winnipeg Blue Bombers hoodie. "Gorgeous day."

"I can't believe how stunning your province is!" he blurted out.

"I know, right!" I said, filled with pride. It really was the kind of late summer maritime idyll that lulls unsuspecting prairie folk into believing it's always like this.

Next to the steep wooden staircase leading down to the cove, I spotted a grassy pocket bordered by woods. Perfect. Half-concealed, trustworthy trees, room to lodge the Ox, maybe too close to the cliff edge though...no, it would work. Touchy on the hammock entry, but once inside, pure suspended gold. I glanced down through the trees and made out the infamous opening where rum runners stashed their contraband liquor during Prohibition days. *There will be no keg of rum stashed here tonight*, I chuckled to myself, *only a bleary-eyed cyclist.*

I wasted no time setting up, and when a couple walked by on their way to the lookoff, I just smiled and waved as if I had permission. One kind lady even offered me supplies — she'd been partying at the Over 55 Games in Yarmouth — and I gladly accepted, receiving a gift of two peaches, two yogourts, and a bottle of blue Gatorade. Good thing, too, because all I had left was one boil-bag meal of pasta and enough water to boil coffee. With that manna from heaven, my dream overnight was ensured.

To burn the last stretch of day before sunset, I brought out my fins and snorkel for the first time. I lugged them all this way, I reasoned, so it would be wrong not to use them at least once. And it's not every day you have water access to a Prohibition-famous sea cave, right? Wetsuit zipped, I descended the stairs marked *Beach Access & Cave* and awkwardly yanked on the flippers, mask, and snorkel, almost pulling my hair out by the roots. Aside from a family of gawking tourists, I had the cove to myself. I flopped in.

Instantly my world changed, and I stifled a gasp when a big red crab scuttled out from behind a clump of gently waving seaweed, his over-sized claws poised for battle. I took a deep breath to slow my thoughts. Shafts of sunlight illuminated smooth ridges of granite as I floated over, aware of a gentle push and pull but sure of my ability to navigate. As I neared the cave's opening, I had to veer around a large boulder into exposed water, and a wave swamped my snorkel, sending salt water down my gullet. A few frantic spews later, I found a spot to climb out.

The tourists, who were still watching me, must have thought I was mad, so I played up the Creature from the Deep motif, staggering across the slippery rocks with flailing arms, until I could safely remove my flippers. Like all sea caves, this one was dark and very wet and not at all welcoming, but I went in anyway.

Limp yellow seaweed draped the walls above me, confirming that it was somewhere near low tide. Darkness fell as the opening narrowed, and when I reached the deepest point, I looked back. The black walls framed an oval of the most vivid blues and greens I'd ever witnessed, and it took my eyes a moment to see the water and trees of Smugglers Cove in crisp focus.

Before my swim back, I clambered up the ridged cave wall as high as I could and shimmied over to where the late-day sun struck it. My instinct was to spread my arms wide, and in my black wetsuit I must have looked like a cormorant sunning himself, wings blasting out to soak in maximum warmth.

Back at my cliffside dwelling, I was 84 per cent confident that I'd be alone for the night, better odds than the majority of my previous nocturnal exposures. I changed into dry clothes and carted my kitchen box, my water, my poncho, and my notebook to the chain link fence guarding the cliffside, remembering to stuff my mini copy of Slocum's tome in my back pocket. After placing everything on the long grass past the fence, I hopped over and laid the poncho on a flat spot next to a spire of granite lined with oddly tropical-looking plants. As the kettle boiled, I watched the sun ease slowly down on the glassy sheen of St. Marys Bay and send a radiant orange beam across the expanse. *What beauty*, I thought. *And no bugs. Sweet mercy.*

In the last indigo light, I turned to *Sailing Alone Around the World*, looking up often to sight Brier Island in the distance as I followed the *Spray* into the most dangerous waters on Earth, the unforgiving strait we call Magellan.

"On February 11th the *Spray* rounded Cape Virgins and entered the Strait of Magellan. The scene was again real and gloomy; the wind, northeast, and blowing a gale, sent feather-white spume along the coast; such a sea ran as would swamp an ill-appointed ship." Huge, confused seas, omnipresent williwaws (surprising compressed gales), and impenetrable walls of craggy rock lay ahead. Like a big-wave surfer paddling hard to catch the mountain of the day, Slocum knew full commitment was required. To readers, he comes across as fearless, reckless even, but his full trust in the *Spray* and his hard-earned experience in those demanding waters gave him the confidence to send it.

One spin of the desktop globe will tell you all you need to know about Cape Horn: it is the only point of land brash enough to occupy the latitudes known as the Furious Fifties. Here, wind and water that rush unimpeded in a whirling global cycle encounter rock, and the land itself hooks away from the ceaseless current. After Magellan and Drake somehow made it through, Charles Darwin quivered in fear as *The Beagle*, the famed ship he was naturalist on, had a go. "Any landsman seeing the Milky Way," he noted, referring to the breaker-studded waters of Bahía Nassau, "would have nightmares for a week."

What marks Bahía Nassau as the world's most treacherous sailing waters is not necessarily the dozens of tiny mine-like islands, but the refraction of giant swells from Drake's Passage, a sloshing effect created by immovable granite fjord walls. Waves rebound and collide with surprising speed, tossing boats around like rubber ducks in an agitated bathtub. The winds, equally demented, can seem to whip from every direction all at once. In the Milky Way, fear and nausea dominate, and Slocum would need more than skill to survive it. "Great piles of granite mountains of bleak and lifeless aspect were now astern," Slocum wrote, "on some of them not even a speck of moss had ever grown. There was an unfinished newness to the land."

His passage tested every ounce of resolve he could muster. Fierce gales, clutching kelp, and Fuegian pirates kept him awake around the clock. When an old salt in Punta Arenas gave him a box of thumbtacks to sprinkle on deck at night, Slocum knew exactly why. His favourite anecdote became the legend of how the upturned tacks caused a crew of barefoot pirates to abort their boarding mission, buying him time to come out and fire his pistols in the air, scaring the marauders off, Yosemite Sam style.

One sequence of events stands out as Slocum's closest brush with death on his round-the-world voyage, an unbelievable escape he called "the greatest sea adventure of my life," adding, "God knows how my vessel escaped."

His first attempt to clear the Horn and find the favourable Pacific trade winds turned into a four-day ordeal of hellish backtracking. When the wind shifted to a hurricane-force headwind, he had no choice but to reef sails and run southeast. Somehow he found a way to enjoy it. "There the *Spray* rode, now like a bird on the crest of a wave, and now like a waif down deep in the hollow between seas—and she drove on." Giant seas thrilled him; it was land that posed a mortal threat.

By nightfall of the storm's final day, his sails ripped to shreds, he sighted land. In pitch darkness, facing fierce hail and sleet, he was "immediately startled by the tremendous roaring of breakers ahead on the lee bow." The roiling whitewater turned out to be the Milky Way. For that infinitely long night, Slocum gripped the wheel and gritted his teeth, the metallic taste of blood from his ice-slashed face reminding him that he was, against all odds, still alive.

"Slocum's Luck," he called it. There was no other explanation for how, come daybreak, he and the *Spray* were still afloat. Weeks later, after a total of five attempts, he finally cleared Cape Horn into favourable winds that whisked him north out of harm's way. "In a bleak land is not the place to enjoy solitude," he wrote. The date was April 14, 1896, a solid sixty days since he'd entered the Patagonian gauntlet.

After my rare undisturbed hammock slumber, I clambered back over the fence to my perch on the edge of Slocum's "old cruising grounds." The rippled surface of St. Marys Bay spoke of a tranquil morning, and I propped myself to absorb the first rays of sun on my back. A leisurely half-day's sail would take me over to enigmatic Brier Island, where I sensed a secret or two might be revealed. I consulted my map to see what kind of Ox-driven detour I would have to take to get there by land. To consider the route, I had to dig out another page and overlay it, creating a kind of mutant map. My inchworm measurements yielded a ballpark prediction: as the crow flies, Smugglers Cove to Brier Island was 15-ish kilometres, but by road, because of its convoluted shape, the distance ballooned to at least 130 kilometres.

I slapped my throbbing knees and said, "It's your time." To make Brier Island in three days, I'd have to push.

But first, the glorious morning. A flock of crying gulls cruised high above as I plunged the French press and took out my notebook for a scribble. I wrote about how I could see Slocum's boyhood home, how the cut in Digby Neck to the north had to be Petit Passage separating the mainland from Long Island, how I agreed with Slocum that stillness of the mind and deep contemplation are best cultivated in fair weather and solitude, how his perseverance in the Strait of Magellan was a model to follow in life. Gushy stuff, really. I finished by mentioning that I had plans to find the Redneck Psychic, in the off chance that she might dial into a frequency I hadn't found yet.

After I'd slurped the dregs, I stood and stretched my arms directly up to pop my spine, inhaled a lungful of fresh sea air, and held it until an explosive exhale brought me right back down on the poncho. The warming rays worked to bubble up some homesick emotions, and I searched my memory to recall how it felt to hug Genny and the girls. A few more days, I knew, and we'd be together again. Soothing heat poured into me then, and I laid back, closed my eyes, and uncoiled my nerves completely.

That's when The Plan came to me, fully formed, almost like a vision. I sat up and grabbed my notebook to capture it before my rational brain could shoot it down. Here it is, just as it appeared in my notes.

The Plan

Fact: Joshua Slocum was the first person to sail around the world single-handed.

Future Fact? I will be the first person to paddle a surfboard from Long Island to Brier Island.

The two feats are comparable, right? Novel...yes. Reckless... yes. Pointless...some might say. Ego-driven...of course! Why else be the first to do something? No shame in going for a claim to fame.

Yes, everyone will say it's nuts, stupid, the tide race through Grand Passage is way too swift. But, as Josh would attest, it's all about studying the ocean and knowing its forces and moods.

On the map there appears to be one pinch point between the two islands on the northern opening. I could stash the Ox at the ferry terminal, stock my dry bag with gear for the crossing, launch at "slack

low," paddle my heart out to get across, climb out, switch to hiking
clothes, walk to the ferry terminal on Brier, take it back to Long
Island, restage the Ox, and slip back over to Brier for an afternoon of
exploring and maybe surfing…

Things that Could Go Wrong &
What to Do About It

What happens if I'm taken by the current in a direction I can't con-
trol? The Fundy Tide race is the strongest in the world, so I'm sure
it runs through that gap at a big clip. I should try to find someone
to watch me from shore, a lookout, ideally with boat access. Barring
that, I must at least intelligently and with observable data select and
predict the most likely drift course and launch with that in mind.

So, I need to (a) watch the channel at low tide the day before and
take notes and (b) be sure about tide times and launch in the best
possible window, taking into account perceived duration of crossing
by paddle strength. Then, when I feel good, go and don't look back!

To fill the last few lines on the page, I wrote The Plan in crooked
bubble letters, stippled each letter with dots, and wrote "Would Slocum
Approve?" in my curliest cursive.

There it was, staring up from the lined pages of my battered log.
The Plan, I knew, was a seed planted in my unconscious by the pages
of *Sailing Alone Around the World*. Writing it down made it real. I shut the
notebook like a clamshell and stood up, suddenly ready to move again.

"Now I have a crazy plan," I said to the Ox, as I hooked his last
bungee on. "Are you ready for one last adventure?"

As if on cue, a squirrel at head height let go a series of chirps so sharp
I jumped. "I'll take that as a yes?"

And with adventure on my mind, I eased back onto the Evangeline
Trail, blissfully unaware that The Plan would not be the only risky prop-
osition to come my way on the wild French Shore ahead.

Chapter 11

BAD DECISIONS

All living beings, without doubt, are afraid of death.
— *Sailing Alone Around the World*

"Dere he is..."

"Looks like he's done dis before..."

"Shine d'light over dere..."

For a drawn out second, I thought the voices might be focused on someone else, but what other silly person would be camped in the bush next to a cemetery? Then a flashlight beam hit me, and I froze as the canvas lit up, revealing my body cloaked in a blood-red sleeping bag, my Dracula-esque shape animating the translucent cocoon.

I'm getting busted, I thought, *it's finally happening.*

"Come out, please." The deep voice carried a French accent.

"Coming!" I yelled back.

In a flourish that must have looked like a butterfly emerging from a larval sac, I struggled with the zipper on my sleeping bag, ripped open the Velcro seam, and swung my legs out. The beam held steady on my face; I squinted back.

"Can we see some identification?"

"Uh...," I stammered, "yes, yes of course."

A nest of sharp sticks jabbed my bare feet, but I couldn't move. I made out an RCMP truck and three dark figures standing in a row, each one shining his flashlight in a different direction, Hollywood premiere style.

"Now, sir," came a much firmer voice.

That got me moving. I fumbled for my wallet, pulled out my licence and held it up for inspection. A shrouded phantom snatched it away.

"What's your story?" came next.

Having been yanked from the brink of sleep, my answer was slow to arrive, but then it all gushed out of me. I'd never heard my voice whimper like that. I told them I was a teacher on sabbatical, that I was happily married with two kids, that I was on a harmless quest, and that I would be gone by sunrise the next day.

A long silence followed. I was tempted to fill it with more proof, any proof that I was not an escaped fugitive on the lam.

"Well, sir," the good cop said, "we can see you have a cozy campsite here, but we received a complaint from d'apartment building back dere, and dat's why we're here now. Can you understand why someone might find your presence…alarming?"

"Oh," I said. "Oh ya, I guess, I mean, ya, I guess."

I could see the officer who took my licence punching keys on a dashboard computer. Behind the truck was a forest of tombstones bathed in moonlight, a big Christ-on-the-cross standing watch. I took my first conscious breath and felt the cool night air fill my lungs.

Indeed, I was being busted by the cops, it was really happening. And I was in my pajamas, in a jagged swath of pine trees strewn with discarded funeral flowers, beside a gravel cemetery access road, across the street from the Université Sainte-Anne in Church Point. I pictured my upcoming night behind bars and wondered if they'd at least let me change out of my PJs first.

The officers huddled together and spoke in a hushed franglais, periodically shining a light at me as I shivered in the deepening cold. By the time they turned my way, I was ready to plead guilty to whatever charge they wanted to throw at me.

"Here's your card," the stern cop said, thrusting it my way. "You know you can't camp here, eh?"

I nodded vigorously.

"And you know dis is trespassing?"

More tremulous nods.

"Well…," he took a long pause, "we'll let it go if you pack up and move."

"Of course," I said, relieved.

They stood there staring at me.

"Oh," I said, "like right now."

"Ya, right now."

And so it was that I strapped on my headlamp, untied all four knots, removed all four pegs, gathered up the blown parachute mess, packed everything back together, and mounted it on the Ox, the Church Point RCMP as spectators.

Seeing as I had no place to go, the good cop was kind enough to recommend a spot behind the university where I could shelter for the night, so that's where I headed as their truck crunched away. I sincerely hoped it would be the last time I cycled through town, any town, in my jam-jams.

"Bad Decisions" is not just a Strokes song, it's a way of life. From my monkish morning at Smugglers Cove to my forcible ejection that night in Church Point, I'd made several dubious calls that angered my sore legs to the brink of quitting.

The first one came before noon. With the Redneck Psychic firmly in my sights, I veered off the northbound Evangeline Trail at the Meteghan Connector and ran inland toward a dodgy business address I'd found through a quick search on a borrowed laptop at the Lakelawn Motel. The Redneck Psychic and I had made only the loosest contact in the form of an awkward voicemail I left on her phone, so I wasn't acting on an invitation. As I huffed up the day's first hill, I told myself to be bold, face fate, court confrontation. Yes, I would find this enigmatic person, this spiritual medium, and then—well, honestly, I hadn't thought that far ahead.

The address took me to a single-storey office building on a patch of grass with a sign out front advertising *Blue Ridge Signs and Graphics Ltd.* There were only two employees inside, a middle-aged lady out front and a man I couldn't see working in the back. The lady looked at me funny when I mentioned the Redneck Psychic, but then she called, "Roy! This guy's looking for the Redneck Psychic."

"S'dat right," Roy said, popping his head out from the hidden room. He wore a blue ballcap propped up on thick glasses.

"Yes," I replied. "The Redneck Psychic? This *is* her business address?"

Roy and the lady laughed.

"She don't work here no more," Roy said. "She used ta, but now I'm not sure where she is. Probably at her house I'm guessin'."

"Any chance you know where she lives?" I asked, hopeful that she was at least in the vicinity of my route.

"She's far out, dat's all I know," Roy laughed. "Too far out for me. I'm pretty sure she lives in the woods back of Salmon River, off-grid and all dat. Like I say, too far out for me!"

After these good souls humoured me, I hit the road with a major decision to make. Roy said I'd have to go to DJ's Corner Store in Salmon River. Someone there would know how to find the Redneck Psychic. Salmon River . . . it sounded familiar.

"Please don't be a backtrack," I whispered, scanning my latest slice of map. "Oh no," I said, shaking my head, "that's not good." Salmon River was there, all right, but it was all the way back past Mavillette Beach, practically halfway back to Yarmouth.

A finger measurement told me I was looking at a ten-kilometre sacrifice, which would double when I made up the ground. With a car— or even an e-bike—this was a no-brainer, but with the sluggish Ox? Pure lunacy. I had no choice but to unsheathe the Magic 8 Ball from its dusty holster. Before I popped the question, I weighed my thoughts: run the punishing Highway 101 in a headwind for at least ten kilometres, take my chances on finding intel at DJ's, then bike wherever to the Redneck Psychic's house, where she will either not be home or, if she's there, won't appreciate being barged in on by some sunburnt yahoo with an oddball request. I gave the dark orb a gentle slosh and presented my quandary.

"Should I backtrack to Salmon River to find the Redneck Psychic?"

I turned the ball over and watched the little white pyramids twirl in the blue, praying for an endorsement of my indecent proposal. When the triangular face rose up, it said *Outlook Not So Good*.

I looked skyward and sighed. Clearly I was not thinking straight at all, because the next thing I knew, I fastened the 8 Ball to the frame, straddled the Ox, and pointed for the highway.

The irony of forsaking the Magic 8 Ball to search for an invisible psychic was lost on my fried circuitry, and as I merged onto the two-lane ribbon of Highway 101 and took my first futile southbound pedals, I felt like I was giving a middle finger to the universe.

Gusty wind to the face, litter-strewn shoulders, sketchy passes by raging pickups, long uphills, blasting sun — it all mixed together and threatened to extinguish the flickering flame of optimism I nurtured. A gruelling hour later, I saw the exit for Salmon River and took it, fighting back tears of exhaustion and regret. The crossroad pulled me the last kilometre to DJ's Corner Store.

With the syrupy slow movements of an old Western movie cowboy, I extracted myself from the Ox's painful saddle and struggled up the wooden stairs, where I tried for a saloon-style entry. The door barely budged.

My enquiry after the Redneck Psychic set in motion a series of hilarious calls across the shop.

"Y'know Kelley M?"

"Yep!"

"Where's she livin'?"

"Not sure, ask David!"

And soon enough I was seated at a restaurant booth awaiting the cheeseburger lunch special and eavesdropping on a conversation between three animated Acadian men in raucous French.

One of them, Dave, looked over to me and said, "You looking for Kelley M?"

"Yes," I replied, surprised. Somehow he'd gotten the message, likely when I was in the washroom scraping road grime off my face.

Dave and his buds were true Acadian beauties. They chuckled about Kelley, especially when I referred to her as the Redneck Psychic. Dave knew her. In fact, he owned the office building she used to rent. My eyes lit up as he texted her, and, while we waited for a response that never came, I brought my map over and he showed me where she lived. It was not good. Her off-grid cabin was at least fifteen kilometres inland, on a lake accessed by dirt road.

The guys laughed when I asked if I could get there by bike. "Dat's far out, bud."

They were curious about my reasons for contacting her, and Dave's flat response to my airy fairy spiritual Slocum nonsense had us all in stitches.

"I'll save you d'trip," he said, rubbing his temples. "When you get to Brier Island, you will be . . . tired."

Had I given up all those road miles for this prediction? Was this Nostradamus joke squarely on me? Yes, yes it was. I could only eat my delicious burger and chuckle along with the b'ys. They were right, I'd misplaced my mind.

Having heard nothing from Kelley, Dave fired off a few more texts before leaving me alone in the booth to write. I jotted my thoughts, scoped the map, recalibrated, and tried to put any notion of the Redneck Psychic out of my mind. It just wasn't in the tea leaves.

As soon as I'd finished writing "time to give up the ghost" in my notebook, a woman in pale green nursing scrubs flew into the empty dining room, paused, looked at me, and walked right over. Her eyes were magnified by a pair of bifocals and her short-cropped, greying hair spoke of coastal practicality.

"You Ryan?" she said.

"Yes," I replied.

"I'm Liz, Kelley's friend." She held out her phone. "Dave texted me and told me you were looking for her?"

"Oh," I said, leaning forward on my seat, "yes, the Redneck Psychic, yes, I'm looking for her."

She frowned slightly. "She doesn't really use that title anymore."

"Oh."

"My cabin's next to hers. She's an old friend of mine. When I heard someone was lookin' for her, I rushed over here."

The ensuing conversation was bizarre and charged with energy. I shared my goal of channelling Joshua Slocum. Liz told me that Kelley M. had stopped doing psychic readings and gone into hermit mode so a visit from me would likely not be welcome, but she would try to reach Kelley tonight. My phonelessness baffled Liz, but she was game to meet the next day. No promises, of course. A flimsier plan was never hatched, but Liz was keen to give it a go. Mostly she was keen on Kelley M.

"She has a gift," Liz whispered, still standing. "I've seen her channel people before. It gives me the shivers to think about it."

"Thanks again, Liz," I said, "I really appreciate it. So, I'll try to be outside the university library tomorrow morning? And if you don't show, it means you have no news from Kelley for me?"

"I wish you had a phone!" she squeaked. "Oooh, I love a good mystery though."

"Me too," I laughed.

"I guess I'll just cross my fingers that we'll meet again?"

"And I'll do the same!"

When I emerged into the harsh light of another sunny afternoon, the prospect of retracing the coastal road all the way back to Smugglers Cove and beyond was not so sour. I just turned the pedals, that's all there was to do. My ride turned out to be one long Groundhog Day session, highlighted by an old man on his porch who'd nodded at me the day before. There he was, as if he hadn't moved for twenty-four hours. When he saw me, he nodded in identical fashion, totally unfazed by the same surfboard-toting cyclist he'd seen the day before. Days on loop, that's the ticket. I liked his style.

Traffic thickened as I passed through Meteghan proper, with its string of gas stations, a Tim Hortons, and the bustling Harbour Authority chock full of broad-nosed fishing boats. It was glaringly evident that I was in seafood land.

In Saulnierville, I was tempted to hit the Frenchys—Nova Scotia's famous bargain-bin clothing chain—but I hauled on, eager to see if the grand spire I made out way up the coast was the namesake behind Church Point. I willed myself there with enough time to choose a hidden hammock hovel, grab a bite from the chip truck, and hit the sling for a well-earned sleep.

Two final bad decisions were left to be made.

Choosing a cemetery bordering an apartment parking lot as a good place to camp was one of them. In my defence, there were very few options around the wooded university grounds that wouldn't be stumbled on by security guards. I thought the graves might cast enough shadow to obscure me, but clearly I was wrong.

And the finale. As I finished my exploratory tour of the Université Sainte-Anne, with its austere church-like buildings and towering oaks, I rounded the library and passed the only car in the parking lot, a battered red Mazda Miata with the top down. I made eye contact with the driver, an older man with Einsteinian hair, and he honked at me to come over.

"How long ya been on dat ting?" he asked.

"Around twenty days," I replied.

"Twenty days!" he blasted out in a coarse Acadian baritone. "Wow, dat's livin'!"

I laughed. Though I found it a tad strange that he was sitting alone in his car, almost meditating, the man was jovial and full of zest. After I told him about my Slocum search, he got even more jazzed and told me about the love of his life, the sailboat he'd bought back in July.

"Wanna go sailing?" he said, after singing the virtues of his baby.

The question was so out of the blue, so forward, that I just looked at him and shrugged.

"Ya," he said, filling the silence. "I'm goin' out tomorrow, last one of d'year before I pull 'er out. You should join me. If you're in, come to the Saulnierville wharf at noon. Mine's de only sailboat dere."

"Uh, I'll have to think about that. Thanks though."

"Okay. Gotta go now. Nice talkin' wit you. Remember, noon tomorrow, Saulnierville."

Then he fired up his car, backed up, and ripped out of there.

What had just happened? And more importantly, how far back is

Saulnierville again? Another backtrack? To go sailing with that loose cannon? He seemed nice enough, although there was something different about him. Not sinister, just a little…eccentric. Yet if it was my only shot to go sailing, to feel what Slocum felt? A bad decision might be the only one left.

"Death is an inescapable fact of life, but all major spiritual traditions teach that far from being the end, death is a transition to new and grander possibilities." Words straight from the *Essential Guide to the Tarot*, a book my mother gifted me along with my first deck of cards. At the last minute, just as I was leaving my kitchen in Cow Bay, something told me to tape the Death card on the inside of my notebook. As much as I would've preferred to keep that macabre image out of my mind, I heeded the call and hastily stuck it on the blank cardboard.

My response to this grim image was to fill the rest of the page with what my eight-year-old daughter, Rosalie, had said to me the day before, when I was trial climbing the fully loaded Ox up our steep street.

"This is not going to be easy, Rosie," I wheezed.

She responded quickly, wise as an ancient sage. "If you think it's easy, it's easy. If you think it's hard, it's hard."

Placing her words next to the Death card seemed to bring balance to my notebook, even though I had no idea how the two entities meshed.

I've always agreed with Hamlet. He called death "the undiscovered country" and that's truly what it is. We will always and forever view death through a kaleidoscope of different lenses, and the only thing we will agree on is that, as my tarot guide says, death is inescapable. I like inevitable better. And rather than locking the notion of my own death in a cupboard and ignoring it, I'd rather keep it out in the open where it can breathe. Maybe that's the only way I can turn my fear into the most elevated of human characteristics: curiosity.

The Death tarot card is gnarly to look at though. Mine has a yellow-faced skeleton in armour riding a white horse, his flagstick jutting up to a square black flag with a white rose on it. A piercing sun sets in the distance between two granite towers, and in the foreground there's a dead body covered by a sheet, a Bishop-esque man with hands extended, and two children, one looking away, the other offering flowers. My guide tells me that the Death card "gives us important opportunities to reassess our attitudes to life and death" and that "there is nothing alarming about the card, which is about change and transition." Reassuring, right? With keywords like *transition*, *letting go*, *loss/gain*, *reassessment*, *optimism*, *rebirth*, and *catharsis*, dark first impressions can flip to something sunny, hopeful even. In the twenty days of solitude leading to my night in Church Point, I'd glanced at the card in passing, and my feelings for it seemed to toggle with my mood at the time. On those buoyant bluebird mornings, it made me happy. On those rainy hammock nights, I preferred not to look at it.

After my nocturnal RCMP displacement, I had decided to jot some thoughts by headlamp, and instead of flicking past the card, I shined my light on Skeletor. He was on his horse as usual. As I reached up to flip the page, something appeared on the card that I'd never seen before, something that made my eyes widen. I tried to sit up, which was impossible in the hammock, so I just wriggled around instead, blinking at the tiny revelation. It was a distant sailboat on a river. A single-sailed craft heading downstream with a minuscule black figure at the helm.

Everything I'd read about Slocum's death, one of the world's greatest sea mysteries, sunk back into me. At sixty-four years old, Slocum had deteriorated along with the *Spray*, and most accounts of the stoic captain from 1908 speak to an air of melancholy about the man. Couple this with an actual funk of demise — Slocum had a cache of ripe conch shells aboard — and you have a picture of a lost man in the twilight of a great achievement the world had all but forgotten.

When the fall of 1908 arrived, Slocum sailed from Martha's Vineyard toward the Caribbean with another seemingly impossible voyage in mind: he would sail up the Orinoco river in Venezuela, across the Rio Negro, and down the mighty Amazon River back to the Atlantic. The last time anyone saw Slocum alive was in Miami, where he brought the dilapidated *Spray* into dry dock for repairs.

Stan Grayson, my favourite Josh biographer, answers his own question: "What was the event that ended Joshua Slocum's life? It is unlikely that the circumstance will ever be known." Grayson favours the theory that the *Spray* was run down by a steamship at night while Slocum slept below, citing a 1959 newspaper report that offered fresh, yet somewhat unreliable, evidence supporting it. What else might have claimed his life? Some believe he and the *Spray* were lost in a raging storm. Some say he tied up at a remote Caribbean island, disguising his identity to make a fresh start. And some, like his son Garfield, preferred to think he shaped his own conclusion.

"Father told me that he wanted to be buried at sea," Garfield said, "and he got his wish."

The sailboat on my Death card was either a coincidence or a sign, so I stuck the image in the back of my head next to where The Plan was gestating, switched my mind mixer on, and slipped off to yet another surface-skimming half-sleep.

The deep *click* and *whir* of a labouring wind turbine woke me and spilled me out onto the crusher-dust trail, my body cracking back to life with a sequence of skeletal pops. Where was I? For a few minutes, I had no idea, and I didn't really care. I was here. I was sore. I was hungry. The adventure continued.

After untying my hasty knots and stuffing the Ox full, I walked him out of the thicket and onto a back road that led to the heart of the university campus. To kill some time before the student centre opened, I grabbed the Irving bologna sandwich I'd bought the day before—selected because I'd never seen a thicker slice—and walked a wooded path called Le Petit Bois.

I found myself in a cool cedar grove teeming with zippy squirrels and energized chickadees. And birdhouses, so many birdhouses, each one uniquely built with a picture below it. I stepped close to a red wooden one with a multicoloured rock mosaic on its face. The faded pictures showed a smiling couple, she in a floral dress and he in a white T-shirt with suspenders, standing in front of a large white house. The background was so bleached I couldn't tell if it was ocean or farmland or just sky. A dedication, handwritten in black Sharpie on the wooden frame, read, "Annie & Arcade d'la Light, 1920–1988 & 1915–1982: RIP." I realized this part of Le Petit Bois was a memorial path — I was surrounded by death yet again.

With the hum of forest life permeating the leafy canopy, I saw the place as an antidote to the chillier, more exposed rows of cold cemetery stones. I took note. Honouring the dead with nature felt better to me. Tombstones are overrated; give me a decorated birdhouse any day.

There was no way Liz would show up. That's how I felt after nursing my camp coffee on a bench outside the student centre for a full hour. My connection with the Redneck Psychic was vaporous at best.

I decided to move on, and as soon as I heard the front doors unlock, I stepped inside and convinced the sleepy student at the welcome desk to let me make a call. That made everything better. The home front was in good shape. After catching up, Genny and I made our final plans to meet on Brier Island in exactly three days. There was no wiggle room because that day was Hazel's tenth birthday, a milestone I wouldn't miss even if I were kidnapped by some Acadian madman and chained to a wall. My unscheduled existence was coming to a close, and I felt almost ready to trade it back.

Against the Magic 8 Ball's wishes yet again, I'd decided to follow my gourmet breakfast with a backtrack to Saulnierville to accept the Mazda Miata man's sailing offer, even if it meant that my final road day would be three times as long as any on the journey so far. If it turned out to be a bad decision, I just hoped I'd live to tell about it. Any shot at losing my sailing virginity had to be taken.

Before leaving the student centre for good, I was drawn into a quiet room teeming with well-lit historical signs. Heaven! It was a museum dedicated to Acadian history, and I soaked up every translated word. I learned that the Church Point region acted as a kind of Acadian capital because the local land held the first resettlement seeds, and it was here that the new Acadian flower bloomed from the soil of utter hardship.

I let the confusing fumes of dusty Catholicism permeate me before rounding the final bend, where I almost ran into a display that stole my breath. It was a simple pine coffin, its lid partly askew.

"Don't tell me there's a body in there," I whispered. My fear melted when I noted how similar the lid's shape was to my surfboard. *Here I lay me down to shred...*

"Ryan?" a voice called.

Wait, what? Was I hearing things? I leaned closer to the coffin, cocking my head like a parrot.

"Ryan?"

"Yessss?" I called out.

I heard some shuffling, and then a woman came whipping around the corner. I jumped back.

"Ryan!" she said, her eyes wide.

"Oh, Liz! Hi!"

"I knew I'd find you here. I saw your bike, and the guy out front pointed me here and...now I'm here!"

"Wow," was all I could muster.

Out of her scrubs, Liz resembled most of the ladies I'd seen in the area: sensible jeans, wool cardigan, thick glasses.

"I have a story for you," she said.

"You do?"

"Yes!" She looked around to make sure we were alone. Her voice assumed a conspiratorial quality. "I talked to Kelley, just now. I had a real hard time gettin' her on the phone, so I tried one last time on my way here and she picked up! And she knew all about your guy—what was his name again?"

"Joshua Slocum?"

"Yes, Slocum! So do you want to hear what she told me? She received a message right away, right away."

"A message? What did she say?"

I followed her gaze down to the cockeyed coffin. Then Liz laid it down.

"So, the story goes...Kelley felt that it was warm water, very warm water, not the cold Atlantic. Yes, warm water, and he was in a boat that was not in great shape—there was a time when he thought he should turn back—um, but the locals from the area—yes, locals—the locals took him and sunk his boat. They were angry about something,

something about feet — and she picked up...yes, she picked up a sense of real stinky smelling clothing — and, they were angry, angry about the feet, she doesn't understand why — and..."

I stood in shock, stunned by this uncanny message. "Go on," I said, leaning in.

"And...," she whispered, "they boarded his boat, took him, sank the boat and..."

"*Yes?*"

"They...they killed him."

"What?" I cried.

"They *killed* him," she said with grave finality.

After we'd both calmed down, I told Liz how Kelley's message was all too plausible, how Slocum's boat carried a pungent stench of unclean conch shells, how he was certainly in warm waters, the Caribbean in fact, most likely off Haiti, and how he had a habit of sprinkling thumb-tacks on deck before going to sleep. That might explain the feet and the anger. Maybe someone tried to board the *Spray*, stepped wrong, and took revenge...it was plausible.

"You're the conduit," I said.

"I know!" she replied. "Isn't it cool. I told ya, I love mysteries."

And that's how we left it. Next thing I knew I was alone with the coffin again. I grasped at the story, but it was like a rambunctious puppy in my brain, drawing me in and bouncing off before I could get hold of it. Then a scene leapt to mind, a violent flurry of sand and swords, but Slocum wasn't there. It was his forerunner, Ferdinand Magellan. I'd read about his death at the hands of angry Philippine warriors in 1520; he'd overstepped his bounds and paid with his life. Could Slocum have endured a similar fate?

Boarding a sailboat became essential, I felt, something I absolutely had to do before this raw news would settle. After thanking the student at the desk, I pushed through the glass doors into the sun and strode to the Ox, raring to make another bad decision.

"To Saulnierville!" I shouted. "I mean...back to Saulnierville!"

Chapter 12

DANNY, CHAMPION OF THE WORLD

I had taken little advice from anyone,
for I had a right to my opinions in matters
pertaining to the sea.
— *Sailing Alone Around the World*

I still knew so little about sailing. The books were entertaining, but they swamped me with jargon so often that I took to skimming the tough bits. Sure, I knew *starboard* and *port, bow* and *stern,* and words like *keel, boom, mainsail,* and *jib* called up pictures in my mind. I knew how bad it was to *run aground,* and I got the concept of *sea-room.* But the stuff I didn't know formed a mysterious ocean below me, vast and full of confusion. Words like *clew, abeam, abaft, jackstay, transom, hank, genoa,* and *windlass* offered no visual purchase. What did it mean to *fend off, pitchpole,* or *come about?* And weren't *hiking* and *reaching* members of the rock-climbing lexicon?

The margins of my pocket copy of *Sailing Alone* were stained with inky question marks. What I needed was some real-world experience with a seasoned seafarer who knew what he was doing. Someone with answers. A sailing master.

Danny Leblanc, the man in the rusty convertible, was not that sailor.

A pungent wall of fishiness assaulted my nostrils as I rolled down the gravel toward a clutch of industrial seafood plants in a weedy parking lot wasteland. In the distance I could see an immense breakwall forming a sheltered hook for the couple dozen boats tied up. A pillowy duvet of cloud played canvas to the cartwheeling seagulls as they surfed the eddies of a stiff onshore breeze. Most of the boats flew flags but none were Canadian. As I coasted closer to the single wooden pier, I passed a few dusty pickups and a lone RCMP cruiser with two cops inside. A makeshift office trailer marked the pier's entrance, and its flags matched the others: a red cross on white with a star above and a crescent moon below. Mi'kmaw flags. Saulnierville wharf was home base for the Indigenous fishery.

"Ahoy!" came a growly voice from somewhere down the pier. Danny poked his head out from behind a piling, his Tilley hat tied tight under a snowy white beard that set off a jolly red face scored with deep smile lines. He lay on his back in the shade, bare feet propped up, his lime-green T-shirt pulsing fluorescence. "Welcome to Saulnierville!" he boomed. His belly laugh, which followed him everywhere, marked him as a kind of seabound Santa.

All I could do was wave back.

Ropes of every colour criss-crossed the long pier, bound to fishing boats bobbing two-deep, each dance-floor-shaped deck festooned with lobster traps, Tim Hortons cups, deflated buoys, and upturned buckets. This was not a fastidious place; it was a working wharf. That's why Danny fit right in. Aside from his neatly tucked shirt, everything he owned seemed on the verge of chaos.

"Glad ya came, Ryan," he said. "Here she is, the only sailboat in Saulnierville."

His boat was sandwiched between three fishing vessels. I could tell he was proud of her, but it was also abundantly clear that seaworthiness was her best trait. She floated, but she wasn't pretty. Her green hull wanted paint, her dirty white deck needed swabbing, and her wooden sideboards cried out for sandpaper. Still, this twenty-four-foot sloop was Danny's pride and joy, his baby, and I wasn't about to criticize the man's boat care.

"So what's her name?" I asked, after tripping over a water-filled wine jug on my dank cabin tour.

"Oh, no name yet. I just got her in the spring, eh? This is my first time goin' out without her old owner. I'm thinkin' of namin' her *My Ship Came In* because she changed my life."

"Nice," I replied, suddenly aware that an unnamed boat captained by a fledgling sailor had to be some kind of bad omen double whammy.

"We got half an hour before my buddy Ernie gets here. Let's go get yer bike put away. Y'probably shouldn't leave it out."

"Right, sounds good."

As we walked down the pier, a group of young guys in hoodies and sweatpants arrived carrying buckets. Danny boomed a "Hello!" to each one of them and they grinned back. Clearly the local fishermen saw him as the harmless eccentric that he was.

"Dose guys have a friggin' tough life," he said to me as we hit gravel. "Why can't dey fish? Dey have a right to it. D'friggin treaties say it clear." Danny's Acadian accent seasoned each phrase. "Dese guys just barely make a livin', while the commercial guys make real money. I feel for dese guys here."

As I knew from the newspaper articles I'd read the previous year, Saulnierville was a flashpoint for the dispute between Mi'kmaw fishermen and the mostly Acadian commercial fishermen. Since the Indigenous fishery launched the year before—outside the legal season sanctioned by the federal government—blockades had gone up on both sides, tensions had flared, and a few trucks and even a lobster plant in Lower West Pubnico had been allegedly burned by commercial fishermen furious at the Mi'kmaq for "fishing illegally." From the comfort of my kitchen in Cow Bay, the parade of news articles melded together, and the issue seemed too complex to untangle. Conservation of lobster stocks appeared to be the core of the strife. Mi'kmaw treaty rights said they could fish all year, but commercial fishermen had to follow the rules set out by the Department of Fisheries and Oceans. The only thing both sides could agree on was that the federal government had fumbled the ball. Saulnierville became a powder keg; RCMP cruisers were now permanent fixtures.

"Let dese guys fish!" Danny barked. "Dat's what I say. Y'know d'Indigenous fishery only accounts for 1 percent of de total catch? It's peanuts compared to de big commercial fishers. Dey say it's about con-servation, what a joke. Know what it's really about?"

"No," I said, "what's that?"

"Greed! It's all about greed, friggin' greed for d'friggin' cash."

When we got to Danny's battered blue van, I smiled. Another well-loved vehicle. As I broke down the Ox into his various parts, Danny propped the back hatch open with a two-by-four and cleared the debris so I could slide each piece in like Jenga blocks, making sure to place the Tombstone gently on top. Seeing the Ox in pieces gave me a solemn, funereal feeling. I shared my misgivings with Danny.

"All's well, Ry!" he reassured, slamming the hatch. "Let's go sailing, eh?"

Back at the boat, Danny buzzed around in search of a life jacket for me, stopping to chat with the crews preparing to go out for the day. Cigarette smoke and diesel fumes choked the air, and I felt an urge to be at sea. As Danny tossed me the borrowed jacket, he looked over my shoulder. "Ernie! Hey Ernie, welcome, welcome."

A wiry man wearing dark sunglasses and a sober expression came striding down the pier. He looked to be the same age as Danny, which I'd found out was seventy-three, though his equally white beard was more chiselled than Danny's bird's nest.

"Ry, this is Ernie," Danny said.

I said hello.

"Hi there," Ernie replied in a nasally Maine accent. "So this is our crew for the day then?"

"Dat's right," Danny chuckled, "d'blind leading d'blind!"

Ernie raised his eyebrows, and we all climbed aboard, eager to embark on what was to be a slapstick adventure of Three Stoogian proportions.

Clouds scudded north as we motored through the wharf's narrow mouth, Danny gripping the tiller and Ernie standing stiff, his hand pressed to his forehead like an ancient navigator. St. Marys Bay was alive with wind chop, but the boat cut through easily, her prow jumping up and down as we pointed in the direction of distant Brier Island. I asked Danny if he thought we'd hoist the sails, not knowing if the conditions were right for sailing.

"Course!" he called across the engine's roar. "Sailing by motor's like surfing in a swimming pool!" He let out a piercing seagull cry and a whoop that woke Ernie and me up.

On our way out, Ernie told me about his sailing experience as a boy in Maine, how he'd owned boats but was now living the frugal retired life on a limited pension. According to Ernie, sailboats were money pits, and it was much better to be friends with someone who owned a sailboat. His reticence dissolved as we forged into open water. I gathered that sailing was his elixir of peace too.

"Today Ern's de captain!" said Danny.

Ernie scoffed. "But it's *your* boat!"

"Yeeeooo!" was Danny's unmeasured response.

It took some time for the dynamics to iron out, but Ernie soon realized that Danny, though brimming with enthusiasm, hadn't been the shot-caller on board yet, so when the engine was cut, Ernie gave Danny and I gentle orders to prepare the mainsail for hoisting.

As I steadied the wooden boom, Danny untied the ropes holding the blue sail cover in place. Once it was balled up, the sail was ready to rock. I kept my eyes on Danny as he fiddled with a screw-down clip, which he undid, releasing a metal line. Something caught his attention and he let the line go before attaching it to the other clip. Ernie let out an "Oh no…" and we all watched as the metal line flew up the mast, swinging so wildly that it got tangled with a bunch of other lines way up there.

I looked at Danny. His eyes were saucers.

"Dat's not good," he said.

"Not good at all," echoed Ernie.

After a calm discussion, which I stayed out of, it was decided that our best course of action was to return to the wharf. My spirits sank. Would I not get to actually sail? I masked my disappointment and sat quietly on the prow, gripping the handline and watching the white caps shimmer in the sun. Danny was more subdued, knowing that his blunder might cost us a day of sailing.

The tide was near full when we nudged up against the pier to trouble-shoot our tangle. Danny and Ernie used a long hook to jostle the metal clip, but in futility: the fouled lines were too high up the mast. If we were six hours earlier or later, the boat might have been low enough to reach the mess from the wharf.

"Guess we gotta let the tide drop before we can reach it," Danny said finally. "Better have some grub."

He ducked into the cabin and came back with a fresh loaf of banana bread wrapped in wax paper, which he tore into three hunks and passed around. His daughter had baked it for him, he proudly announced. "She takes care of me."

"It's delicious," I said, "thank you."

I chewed and looked up at the fouled mess. *Maybe I'm not meant to sail yet*, I thought. There has to be a reason for this. I cast my mind to Slocum, and there he was, staring at me with those hard, self-reliant eyes, his shiny dome and imposing goatee aglow. *You're the one who has to fix this*, he seemed to say. *You'll have to climb up there.* Climb? Seriously? *Dead serious*, Slocum's face conveyed. *If you want to sail, you must climb.*

"Guys," I piped up. Danny and Ernie were deep into a bag of bar-beque chips, but they stopped to look my way. "Guys...I think I can climb up there."

They both looked up. Danny let out his biggest laugh of the day. "Normally I'd say no way," he said, "but what de heck. I get good feel-ings from ya, Ry. It's crazy, but if ya tink ya can do it, I say go for it!"

"But be careful," Ernie added. "That's at least three storeys high."

As I stood at the base of the aluminum mast and tested the metal line running down it, I noticed a crew of fishermen looking at me from their boat. So I had an audience. Excellent. But it seemed possible. I'd always loved climbing those rafter ropes in gym class, and I'd spent a good deal of my teenage years climbing trees. I was also feeling spry from my twenty-day fitness freak out.

"I got this," I whispered.

Both hands taut on the metal line, I gripped the mast with the insides of my faded Converse and started shimmying, each upward jerk bringing me closer to the T-shaped crossbeam where I planned to stand. I resisted the temptation to look down, and with quivering forearms I pulled until I was close enough to grab the T and scramble up to my feet. Only then did I look back. The lobster boys were shocked.

One guy, exhaling a cloud of smoke, said, "You'd never catch me doin' dat!"

Danny and Ernie were silent, but they were beaming. I reached up and got hold of the lost clip. From there I had to gently throw it out and catch it with my other hand, all the while keeping a grip on the mast. One, two, three times I swung the line, until I got it free and fed it back down to Danny, his arms outstretched to catch it. Once I was sure we were solid, I thought for a split second of jumping the twenty-five feet into the water. If I wasn't in my only accessible set of dry clothes, I would've gone for it. Instead, I re-gripped with raw hands and carefully slid down the mast until my feet touched deck.

"Holy frig, Ry," Danny said, "ya saved d'friggin' day!"

"Impressive," Ernie chimed in.

And just like that, we headed back to open water for another shot at running under wind power. A glow of pride rose in me, but I tried not to show it. Danny was effusive, calling out bizarre expressions like *piece a cake-o, a'right*, and *rub a dub dub!* to the wind. He embodied the wild sailing spirit, and there was no place he felt more alive than out to sea on his boat, where land-based worries evaporated and only the moment remained.

As things settled, I told Ernie about my interest in Joshua Slocum. He nodded knowingly.

"I'll tell you," I said, "Slocum had lots of problems to solve out there."

"Solo sailing," Ernie responded, "guaranteed you're gonna have problems. When you're alone they're much, much worse."

He told me all about a guy he knew who built a Tancook Whaler down in Alabama, how he had attempted to sail it solo around Florida and up the eastern seaboard for Nova Scotia, and how he'd hit a squall off Cape Hatteras that kept him at the wheel for four straight days.

"Weird stuff happens to you," he said. "By day four you're hearing voices."

The guy had to scuttle his plans of sailing to Big Tancook Island. Most solo voyages, I learned from Ernie, didn't succeed.

Danny's boat rocked in the choppy waters of St. Marys Bay as we killed the motor and prepared to hoist the mainsail yet again. We laughed when Danny made a theatrical show of attaching the rogue clip to the metal line, which Ernie told me was called a halliard.

"Halliard!" I cried. "I've seen that word."

"That's one any budding sailor has to know," said Ernie.

With Ernie on the tiller offering directions, Danny and I loosened off the ties on the mainsail to free it for flight. The wind whipped the sail around, and at one point it slapped me in the face, cream-pie style. Danny roared with laughter and helped uncover me. I kept a loose grip on the sail as Danny began pulling the halliard, and that's when I noticed something funky happening with the slot in the mast. As he tugged arm over arm, the plastic sliders attached to the sail came out of the track one by one.

"Danny!" I shouted over the *clink clank*, "look there!"

"Oh frig," he said, "oh frig."

"What is it?" Ernie yelled, craning his head around the chaos to see the problem.

"Ern," Danny barked, "Ern, de clips are comin' out!"

"Oh boy," Ernie responded.

We all stared at the mast. A ring of duct tape that had been jury-rigged to backstop the bottom clip had been worn down and scored. As Danny pulled, the clips popped out like candy from a Pez dispenser, rendering it impossible to hoist the mainsail. I knelt there hugging canvas and cursing my misfortune.

"Looks like we'd better head back to the wharf again," said Ernie.

Danny's face flushed red, but he managed a smile. "Okay Ern, yer right. We'll have to fix dis and try again some other time."

"Great adventure though!" I offered, searching for the positive.

"Ya," Ernie called out, "more than you were expecting, I think!"

With the mainsail wrestled back under ties, Ernie fired up the motor and steered us away from Brier Island and back toward Saulnierville wharf. The view was vast. To the north, the great spire of Church Point stood tall; to the south, the hook of Cape St. Marys poked into the sea. I swung back around and watched the low-lying ridge of Brier Island—Slocum's old stomping grounds—recede from view.

For a few minutes we were silent. Here we were in a sailboat, in ideal sailing conditions, and we couldn't sail. It felt like a crime against Josh. I looked up the mast, and it appeared to puncture a shroud of white. My dream, like that cloud, was skewered.

That's when Danny had the idea of the day, a solution so elegant that I wondered why it hadn't struck him sooner.

"Hey Ern," he said, his brow furrowed, "we...could almost use the jib, couldn't we?"

"Say again?" Ernie called out over the engine's roar.

"The jib! We could use the jib!"

Ernie paused, a rare grin spreading across his otherwise stoic face.

"Ya," he said, "if you trust it."

I hugged the mainsail a little tighter. Could we sail with just the jib? As I recalled, Slocum often altered his sail set-up depending on conditions. The jib was a sail, so why wouldn't it catch wind?

Five minutes of excited bustling later, the jib's winch rang out, a suspenseful *click click click* that made it feel like we were on an ascending roller coaster. Danny muscled the jib up and swung it to the wind, where it instantly filled with air and billowed proudly out. I felt the boat lurch ahead and then—I knew it!—we were sailing.

"Yip, yip, yoooo!" Danny hooted, "Yee! Woo! We're sailing baby! We got out of de swimmin' pool!"

I stood up and punched the air, only to slip back and nearly topple into the gaping cabin hatch.

"God damn, Ry," Danny yelled. "Ernie…look at ya, yer a sailor! Friggin' Ernie! Woo! Yip, yip, yippee!"

Once we had swung and drew a bead on Brier Island, Ernie said it was tea time, and he gestured at me to take the tiller, giving me clear instruction. With the engine cut, the forward motion felt unreal, as if we were drawn by a magnet. I grabbed the smooth wooden bar and then Danny and Ernie were gone below. Just past the mangled mainsail I could watch the triangular jib held taut in the wind. The cross breeze hit us square, and I had to keep my forearm locked to hold our course, but hold the course I did, sailing alone on a beeline for Slocumtown. I fell in love instantly. Soon I hatched a plan to buy a sailboat, learn to sail it, and take Genny and the girls down to the Caribbean for a winter of island-hopping. Classic first-time sailor thoughts. But the joy was real, and when Ernie emerged and scanned our line, he offered a compliment that meant more to me than he will ever know.

"Steady line, Ryan," he said. "You're a natural helmsman."

Natural helmsman? In Ernie's eyes? I almost melted with joy.

When it came time to pass the tiller, I crab walked to the bow and rested with my back against the mast, basking in the ecstasy of sailing. Suddenly Slocum made sense. I recalled a line from when he crossed the Pacific and nodded my head: "I was en rapport now with my surroundings, and was carried on a vast stream where I felt the buoyancy of His hand who made all the world." Just like surfing. Exactly how I felt while gliding down the face of a wave.

The next hour was a blur punctuated by "yips" and "yees" and seagull squawks from Danny, the Champion of the World. When we returned to the wharf, hauled down the jib, and started the motor, the spell was broken and I slumped back, exhausted. After we'd tied up and Danny had talked to his fishermen buds on the pier, Ernie left us with a "Farewell friends!" We walked back to Danny's van.

The resident RCMP cruiser was still there; Danny waved at the sheepish officers. "Poor buggers. Imagine sittin' where you weren't welcome all day."

Now that I knew what kind of legend Danny Leblanc was, I was ready to accept his generous offer of driving the broken-down Ox and I back to Church Point and just past, to the old trailer he'd been living in while the side of his house was being rebuilt after a kitchen fire. He was back in his house now, so I was more than welcome to crash in the empty trailer, mouldy as it was. Sounded great to me.

With my feet resting on a sea of coffee cups and shredded newspaper, Danny whisked us up the hill and onto the main road leading north from Saulnierville.

"Hey Danny," I said, "know what you should name your boat?"

"No," he replied, "what?"

"*She's Come Undone.*"

Danny boomed out an "Absolutely!" and we sang the Guess Who lyrics in raucous harmony, windows wide open to let the salt breeze course through.

Danny told me about how he'd been a community actor. He'd played Evangeline's father in a show that toured Acadian settlements as far away as Louisiana. He was passionate about Acadian history and the future of what he called "L'Acadie." I knew my time with him was almost done, so I asked him the question that had been nagging me all afternoon, the same one I wrestled with in the wake of Slocum's death revelation.

"Danny, what's the key to life?"

He looked at me and arched his eyebrows. "The key to life is to keep livin' it, man!"

We both erupted. We were sympatico by then. I hadn't laughed that much since I'd left Cow Bay. The lightness permeating me felt real, almost tangible.

Soon enough we were back in Church Point, and I gestured at the cemetery where I'd been busted, saying "That's my cemetery!"

Danny, unprompted, turned to the subject of life's terminus. I perked up.

"Death, man," he said, tapping the wheel. His bushy eyebrows jumped and the creases in his forehead deepened. "It's out dere."

I nodded, not knowing how to follow that mystical truism.

"It's like Emily Dickinson wrote, man," he said, his voice dropping an octave. "Because I could not stop for Death — / He kindly stopped for me — / The Carriage held but just Ourselves — / And Immortality."

"Wow," I said, "that's . . . kind of beautiful."

"Yessir," he replied, staring ahead.

Chapter 13

SLOCUM'S LUCK

It is known that a Brier Islander, fish or no fish
on his hook, never flinches from a sea.
— *Sailing Alone Around the World*

The Geological Map of Nova Scotia is awash in pinks and greens and turquoise blues, a paint-by-numbers that astounds in its diversity of rock types, from sandstone to schist to shale. This lobster-shaped almost-island province is an epic mash-up of Earth's forces over deep time. While most of the rock types repeat on the map, there is one snaky slash on the westernmost coast with a deep green colour of its own. Running from the northern hook of Cape Split southwest to Brier Island is a continuous ridge of land made of North Mountain basalt, a 150-kilometre separator with the Bay of Fundy on one side and the rest of mainland Nova Scotia on the other. Roughly 200 million years ago it was the zone of a mighty volcanic eruption that kicked off the break-up of Pangea and helped birth the Atlantic Ocean. If Brier Island is the snake's head, then Digby Neck is the top half of its spine.

The Neck looks like it shouldn't be there, like it should have broken off under the strain of the mighty Fundy tides. Twice a day it withstands the surge of a billion tonnes of water, a greater volume than all the world's rivers combined. But its brittle, skeleton-finger appearance is deceiving. There is a powerful sense of permanency in its staunch basalt core, and, aside from its two oceanic cuts formed by receding glaciers twenty thousand years ago — Petit and Grand Passage — this is a neck that shall never break.

No, Digby Neck cannot be broken. But it certainly has the power to break the physical and emotional spirit of a non-e-bike pedalling, absurd load carrying, stained clothes wearing amateur cyclist intent on traversing it in a single run. From my vantage point on the weedy flats behind Danny Leblanc's trailer/slasher-film set, all that rich geological history compressed down to one hard diamond of truth: it looked friggin' hilly, bud.

As the sun rose behind me, I bombed bug spray on every inch of exposed skin and set to work readying the Ox for his final perform-ance. Up to that morning, he'd been so reliably rock-solid that I had complete confidence in his ability to survive our upcoming marathon. What I'd come to like best about the Ox was his style, his flair for the dramatic. Under his Tombstone topper, he still rocked his corked horn, his frayed Nova Scotian flag, his red ox yoke, his gritty Magic 8 Ball, his "I Love Country Music" licence plate, and Derek the seal skull. Serious hell-weasel vibes. Even his mainframe, the rusty Westclox clock that was a permanent fixture on my periphery, was standing tall. Against all logic and the laws of gravity, its minute hand had made one full sweep of the face since we'd left Cow Bay. Technically, I'd only been away for an hour.

With The Plan growing tendrils in my imagination and Danny's lust-for-life spirit as fuel, I pointed the Ox in the opposite direction of Brier Island and steeled myself for a morning of highway grinding. To warm up, I opted for a low-volume detour through Weymouth and over the meandering Sissiboo River, easing along the misty, deserted roads. When I had no other choice, I joined Highway 101 for the last time and braced for danger in the form of barrelling big-rig trucks. After the first few kilometres of wide shoulder and sane drivers, I found I could breathe easier and even drift into a rhythmic trance, my legs swinging in time like twin metronomes.

A playlist of songs paraded through my head as a tailwind whisked me down the slight grade toward the town of Digby, each tune rising up from the many road days before. Popular hits like "I Get Around," "The Seeker," "I'm On Fire," and "The Boxer" floated in before making room for the bunch of originals I'd crafted in my moments of exhausted inspiration, single-chorus tracks like "New Price on the Lighthouse Route," "Tusket Ford Tough," "Rappie Pie Blues," and my homage to Nova Scotia's litter problem, "Toss Yer Friggin' Tim's Cups." I almost had a bad album's worth by then.

As the highway hewed closer to St. Marys Bay, the ever-present green humps of Digby Neck loomed across the water, thick with wind turbines. A bone-shaking shortcut along the bay's head, where I wolfed an Eat-More and reapplied sunscreen, took me to rural Highway 217, the central nerve connecting the mainland to Long Island and terminating at Brier Island. Yes, there would be a price to pay for my easy start. With all that fructose coursing through my bloodstream, I felt ready to attack The Neck.

The red cliffs arcing ahead told me I was now on new geological terrain. Though my knees burned, I knew they were tough and strong and ready to do battle. At Rossway I rounded a turn and looked ahead to see the road run behind a sandy beach and twist inland in an S-shape that went up, up, and then disappeared in the dense green forest. I took some deep squirts from the bottle, set my teeth, and built as much speed as I could across the flats. As usual, any momentum I'd earned evaporated within a dozen metres of slope, and I had no choice but to crunch through all seven gears until I got to my old friend, first gear, the hill climber.

Head down, I swung my shoulders and pushed my knees as hard as I could to inch the Ox's robust mass forward, heaving breaths to keep my lungs from igniting. About halfway up, the road took a cruel two-degree rise and I had to stand down. Standing down on a hill climb can feel like giving up, but it's not that at all. My body knew it could get to the top; I just needed to tax different muscles to do it. The long and winding push-walk was on.

Hands palming grips, I extended my legs back, put my head down and started urging the Ox forward, locking into a slow walker's pace. Gravel crunched, sweat poured, and the headwind sweetened as I panted into my soaked shirt. When I chanced a look up, a truck flew down the hill and the passenger pointed at me with a shocked expression, as if to say, *Did you see that deranged person?*

Ages later, I rounded what had to be the final bend and saw the road shoot up again. It was the first time I truly felt that I might not make it, that The Plan would have to remain the foolhardy figment that it was. I had nothing left.

I pulled off into the long grass, booted open the kickstand and collapsed on the Tombstone, my face smushed against hot black paint. Sweat stung my eyes and I wanted to cry, to wail, to rage, but the absurdity of that image flipped my script, and I could only laugh and laugh. All at once I knew I had misnamed my cargo bike. It was no ox. It only moved when I gave it my energy. The metaphor was muddled all along. I was the beast of burden, I shouldered the load, I wore the yoke. The bike was more of an ox cart and I, well, I was the Ox.

Somehow, knowing that made me stronger. Oxen were stubborn, oxen never gave up. Sure, they were driven by sometimes ruthless owners, and sure, they didn't have a choice, but they always got it done. My totem of Joshua Slocum held the whip, and he made it clear that I had to get to the tip of Long Island by the end of the day to put The Plan in action. It helped to pretend I had no choice. I felt Slocum's stinging *snap*, and I had to respond.

The rest of the mainland followed a similar refrain: long cruisy downhill, bridge over a river, daunting ascent. I hoofed it up hills at Centreville, Sandy Cove, Mink Cove, Little River, and finally, Tiddville. By the time I reached East Ferry, I was famished and nearly out of water. Word of a convenience store across Petit Passage in the town of Tiverton kept me moving, and I used my last reserves to heave my ox cart onto the car ferry. This was supposed to be the crossing that confirmed the possibility of The Plan, Petit Passage being a similar-sized gut to Brier Island's Grand Passage.

The ferry's diesel heart roared to life, and I compelled my rubber legs to the rail to scan the seething water, its strange swirls like oversized river eddies. Immediately the ferry swept sideways in the current and it had to goose its engines to avoid being swept down the Bay of Fundy drain. The smattering of houses on the shore of Long Island seemed far away, certainly too far to paddle in this kind of colossal rip. *Must be an hour from high tide*, I thought. The whole Atlantic Ocean poured through Petit Passage into the Fundy Basin, completing a twenty-foot sea-level rise in six short hours. I knew that The Plan hinged on one crucial data point: accurate tide times. Launching in water like this oily vortex would be like dropping into maxed-out Pipeline. For expert crazies only.

It had to be mid-afternoon when I made the Tiverton General Store, the first and only food stop between Rossway and Brier Island's single town, Westport. Stanton-the-proprietor, a kind-hearted man with a limp and an open smile, became my saviour in three distinct ways. First, he sold me all the foods: homemade potato salad, a mini pizza sub, a cold-cut sandwich, a can of Starbucks Double Shot, a bag of chocolate-covered espresso beans, and a slice of SKOR cheesecake (for later). Second, he shared vital information: dead low tide in Grand Passage would happen at 8:08 a.m. the next morning. Third, he offered me a place to camp for the night, which happened to be on the shoreline overlooking Grand Passage with a full view of Westport Harbour and the Brier Island ferry route. Though I was careful not to tell him I was thinking of paddling my surfboard across, I did manage to glean some harrowing insight into how Grand Passage worked.

"Water can move at seven to eight knots through Grand Passage," he said. "That's about fifteen kilometres an hour. It's real swift in there."

"Oh," I replied, "so hypothetically, if someone were, say, kayaking across, when would be the best time to do it?"

"Never?" he laughed. "I guess on the hour leadin' to slack low. That's when the current's tamest. Even still, I'd never take the risk."

"Fair enough. Thanks for your help. I might take you up on the camping offer if it's okay with you."

"Oh, have at it! Go past the ferry, and the house at the end is mine. Lots of room to pitch a tent."

"Thank you, Stanton," I replied, "that means a lot."

Long Island is aptly named, I came to learn, but its climbs showed mercy as I pushed south on potato-salad power, rolling over the zebra-stripe shadows cast by roadside spruce in the waning light. This was the route between ferries, which meant I had the road to myself for intervals of fifteen minutes or so, when a bumper-to-bumper string of cars would fly by, intent on making the scheduled ferry times. I reluctantly passed the parking lot for the trail to the Balancing Rock, a twenty-foot freak-of-nature slab of columnar basalt that stands proud on the shore of St. Marys Bay. It was either the rock or The Plan, and I'd made my choice.

As I passed a sign for Freeport and swung down into a colourful fishing village, I made out Brier Island across the turbulent water, the lights of Westport gleaming in the dusk. It was beautiful and it was distant. Too distant? I looked away to avoid rethinking The Plan.

Stanton's land was easy to find, but there was one pressing problem. It had plenty of rocks and wildflowers and grass but no trees over my height. I made the quick and painful decision to go with my tarp-plus-bike set-up and got busy making it liveable. With the sun buried behind Brier, I grabbed my fork and SKOR cake and found a perch overlooking Grand Passage, ready to observe and make a realistic calculation of my chances of paddle crossing success.

It was a solid 300-metre gap. The water coursed through, but with less urgency than in Petit Passage, a function of the approaching slack tide. The opening to Fundy was right there, way too close for comfort, and my intended landing spot seemed to be a craggy wall of seaweed-smeared rock. But that water...I sensed that if I used the paddling strength and stamina I'd built up from years of surfing, I could beat the current at slack tide. It was a gamble, no doubt about it. I stood up for a better view.

"Yes, I can do it," I almost shouted.

"Y'can do wha?" came a voice from nowhere. A young guy carrying a bucket stomped into view, his tall rubber boots squelching water.

"Oh, hey," I said, "uh, nothing. Just dreaming out loud."

He showed me his haul of periwinkles from the evening's forage—little bluish snails, good to eat—and I asked him about the area.

"Ya," he said, propping up his hat and looking toward the ferry, which was halfway across the gut and spinning in the current, "d'water rushes tru' here somethin' fierce."

I asked if anyone had ever, say, swam across? He scoffed. Not in his memory. But there were two scuba divers who drowned the previous year.

"Dey let go dere line and whoosh, dey were both swept out t'sea."

"Oh man," I said, "that's not good. Were they first-timers?"

"Nope," he said, "well seasoned, dey were. Just timed 'er wrong and made a mistake."

Once the kid trudged off, I made the decision to wake early, watch for as long as necessary, and launch at sunrise, a solid hour before low tide. I had no one to bounce my idea off, no one to share my resolve with, but neither had Slocum. What he had was solitude, and solitude nurtured his willingness to trust his instincts.

As I brushed my teeth under the headlamp's beam, I saw how filthy my hands were, I felt how greasy my matted hair was, I smelled how ripe my clothes were, and I knew, more than anything, that what I needed was a cleansing swim. To ward off the bugs, I had one final rough camping brainwave. What if I slept in my hat and pulled the hammock tent mesh taut over my head? I'd be able to breathe, and the mosquitoes would be barred entry. *Yes*, I thought, *let's try that tonight*.

"As would be demonstrated time and again, Joshua Slocum, skilful and determined as he was, sailed with an angel perched on his shoulder. He called it, eventually, Slocum's Luck." In Stan Grayson's authoritative biography, *A Man for All Oceans*, tales of Slocum averting disaster through sheer fortune jump up in the narrative like dandelions. On one of his first voyages overseas, he slipped and fell from the upper topsail yard, but the main yard broke his fall and saved him from plummeting sixty feet to certain death. During his circumnavigation on the *Spray*, a steamship roared past him in the middle of the night, its hull so close he could almost touch it. Off Brazil, he flipped his tiny dory and got hold of the last foot of line to pull himself to safety. And, finding himself completely lost in a treacherous section of Polynesian coral reef, a local pilot materialized out of thin air to guide him. Once he internalized the story that he was a lucky man, Slocum made the decision to fly in the face of accepted seaman superstition and adopt 13 as his lucky sign. This "fatalistic number," as he called it, would become his friend, his darkly humorous talisman.

The great irony in seafaring lore is that a sailor in Slocum's time, while undertaking the kind of mortal risk that would scare the pants off a modern mariner, could not swim. With a wool suit for a life jacket, it's no wonder a plunge in the water spelled doom for the nineteenth-century sailor. When Slocum's dory overturned, he tasted real, metallic fear, even if he downplayed it in his book with this hilarious line: "I suddenly remembered that I could not swim." He feared drowning, and his whole game was to build an arsenal of superior shipbuilding and navigation skills to keep him on deck at all times. And if drowning was his fear, sharks were the terrifying manifestation of it. That's where death lived for Slocum: in the cold, opaque eye of a great white.

Joshua Slocum would have seen surfing as the height of lunacy. To paddle out on a plank of foam into the shark's domain, to dangle one's feet, to present oneself on a platter to the apex predator of the vast ocean he loved—this would have seemed absurd. Slocum liked to joke about his luck, but when it came to risking his life, he was famously calculated.

The camp stove's neon-blue blaze brought the kettle to a violent boil, rattling its cap in the pre-dawn stillness. As I poured the scalding water over my layer of cheap coffee grounds, I strained to find detail in the blackish green wall across Grand Passage. I didn't need trigonometry to tell me that my angle of attack would have to take in the current's force if I were to hit the target.

The caffeinated sludge seemed to help me study, help me think. Sunrise felt a solid hour away, so slack low tide was approaching, and the swirling water appeared almost navigable. Overhead, a ripe full moon flickered on and off as a marbled quilt of cirrocumulus slid past. That meant maximum tides. Max tides in a world of big water. But even a full-moon tidal cycle hits a lull, that brief window when the sloshing water slows before flipping direction and spilling the opposite way. If anything went wrong, the draining tide would pull me toward the docks of Westport instead of into the yawning Bay of Fundy. Observable physics told me that.

I marched back to my tarp for my pre-stocked dry bag and clammy wetsuit, which I pulled on in the cool morning air, its hockey-bag funk twisting my nostrils. The Tombstone looked like a knocked-down monument in its flowery bed, but I knew it was ready. Compared to a session in head-high waves, this mission was a straight shot. I pulled the backpack on, snugged the shoulder straps, hoisted the Tombstone under my arm, and stepped onto the exposed rocks, feeling more like a Navy SEAL than ever. My first slip confirmed that, no, I was not in the special forces. Not even close.

Three full, bruise-inducing bails later, I Velcroed the leash to my ankle and slid the Tombstone into the water, jumping on and pushing out as hard as I could. At first, I paddled frantically, whipping up foam as I urged forward, my mind blankly switching to flight mode. Then it was as if my whole body locked up. I couldn't move, I couldn't think. My left calf cramped first. As I grabbed at it, my right calf followed suit. My other arm shot back reflexively and kneaded muscle. Time seemed to warp and expand around me, conjuring up a drone's vantage: there I was, a contorted crab man on a black surfboard in the bluish predawn, sliding sideways toward the mouth of Grand Passage, the Atlantic Ocean an immense magnet drawing me into a perilous vortex of idiotic, self-imposed doom.

"Calm down, man," I heard myself say, "calm down and concentrate on your strokes."

That seemed to smother my body's electrical fire and I soon found a rhythm, pulling deep with both hands, one after the other, cup and draw, cup and draw. When I rounded the back of an exposed shoal, I took a breathless beat to scan the area. The shoreline of Brier Island looked closer, but I was still moving at a decent clip toward Westport. Something about the current's pace, its insistence, scared me. This time, though, the fear became a catalyst, jolting me back into action. I drew one full breath, dug back in, and got to work.

Near the halfway point, the fear extinguished. My shoulders burned but my craft stayed true. All I had to do was not stop paddling. It was that simple. At the height of my exhaustion, my tired eyes salt-scorched, my muscles flashing pain, I understood Slocum's gift to me: the knowledge that persistence is all.

When I made landfall in a keyhole slot of yellow seaweed-garnished rock, I glanced back to confirm that, indeed, I had followed a cockeyed line across. Not that it mattered. I was touching Brier Island rock in all its slimy glory. I dunked my head in the brine and took a big gulp of saltwater before clambering, Gollum-style, onto the matted bed of kelp, where I splayed out on my back. My stunt was over and all I could do was laugh. It started as a giggle, a kind of call and answer with my inner voice, then it rolled into a more persistent snort, topping out in a triple shot of belly rumblers that left me gasping for breath. Then, I just shook my head.

Now, I swear this happened, and it happened right then. A bald eagle soared into view, high above, turning a wide arc across my periphery. I felt at once it was Joshua Slocum's spirit. At least that's the deeply honest shot of meaning I received in my solitude-soaked bones. It was Captain Solitude himself. Mighty, fearless, solitary, in control, co-opted by Americans and — hahaha, the laughter rushed back into me like a turning Fundy Tide — bald as a Magic 8 Ball.

DEAR JOSH

Guess where I slept last night? Nope, not in the damp, mildewy hammock. Not under the flapping blue tarp. Not on the pressure-treated wood bench outside the tourist office, tempting as it was. I slept in none of those places.

Last night, after a day scouring Brier Island for traces of you, I laid out my kit on ancient planks in a red cedar shake building on stilts above Westport Harbour. I slept right here, Josh, in your father's boot shop. It was a quality sleep too. Now I've pulled an old chair to the dirty window so I can write and watch the rain fall. Hope you'll forgive the intrusion.

Don't worry, I had permission from Vicki and Floyd. They own the shack now. Edna helped me track them down. As you can see, I'm on a first-name basis with the locals already. That's what happens when you take the ferry twice — once on foot, once on wheels — and then criss-cross a tiny island for hours on a highly conspicuous cargo bike.

I rode Water Street. I rode the high street. I stopped at Sweetcake Cove to read your monument and hike the bluff overlooking The Two Gullies. I ran Gull Rock Road to Big Pond Cove, and I pedalled and pedalled and smiled at everyone I met. In a way, you showed me around your old haunts. Thanks for that.

When Floyd let me into your family boot shop he chuckled and told me how his buddy would never, ever sleep here. Claims it's haunted for

sure. I shrugged it off and kept smiling, knowing deep down I was in a
safe place. Even a terrifying Halloween skeleton with glowing red eyes
couldn't rattle me. I took his brittle hand and shook it, introducing
myself. This was dry shelter; I was under a mostly watertight roof. It
would take more than a few dusty cobwebs and ghouls-in-storage to
keep me from my resting place.

A fragment of your past came to me as I lay listening to the water
slosh below. I recalled reading about the time you whittled a sailboat
in secret, in this exact building. It was 1856, and you were twelve
years old. Your father had pulled you from school to learn the boot-
making trade, but you hated the work. Every chance you could, you'd
gaze out the window at the wharves of Westport, dreaming about one
day going to sea on a clipper ship.

When your father found you putting the finishing touches on your
model boat, he snatched it and dashed it to the ground, smashing
yards and masts and stomping his boot on the wreckage.

"Idle hands," he said.

Four years later, at sixteen, you jumped on one of those ships and
left for good.

I fell asleep picturing you there, perched high in the rigging
amongst the taut white sails, your back turned on Nova Scotia as you
chased the eastern horizon.

At the deepest part of my slumber, the sound of a giant wave
ripped me to the surface and I jerked upright. I was at sea! The
rushing water felt so near, so real.

The moment stretched until my eyes fixated on a hole in the
wooden plank beside me and I woke up. High tide again. The hole
was there, I knew, as a pressure valve for storm surges. Your father
probably cut it himself.

Once I knew I wasn't in watery peril, I stepped outside and
onto the midnight wharf. The side of the boot shop danced with
luminescence, a reflection of a reflection from a nearby spotlight
bouncing off the restless water. The moon appeared, framed by a
perfect circle of light. A lunar halo. Like a sign.

If there's anyone who knows what a lunar halo is, it's you. But it
got me thinking. About how you'd become a kind of teacher to me on
my crazy ride from Cow Bay. I'd been searching for your ghost, even
attempted to conjure your spirit, when you'd been there all along. That
book you wrote about taking a little boat around the world by yourself.
Every time I read from it, you're very much alive. Your voice is always
there, waiting to be heard.

I can hear my teenage students saying, "Deep!" Someone usually
does when our class discussion plumbs the philosophical depths. It
always brings us back to the surface, but it's rarely said with derision.
You never minded going deep, Josh. That's something you continue
to teach me. That and self-reliance, pushing myself to wrestle my
own puzzles. But you also teach me to be a keen observer of nature,
the ocean especially, and you teach me to listen to my inner voice.
To navigate by the stars and the moon. I see why you leaned into
solitude. I get it now.

The library on your beloved *Spray* held the books that kept your
mind buoyant as you forded the hundreds and hundreds of quiet days.
You sailed and you read. That's why I brought *Rockbound* and *Bluenose
Ghosts* with me. Those voices from Nova Scotia's past, vivid and
vaporous, somehow magnified yours. And I thank you for introducing
me to new voices, voices of the living and breathing. Mac Morse,
Sandy Hiltz, Danny Leblanc, and all the genuine, wise folks who
showed me kindness down the South Shore and up the French Shore
and down The Neck to right here, your coming-of-age island, the one
they call Brier. Without your call to action, I never would have gone
for it.

[ten minutes later]

Ok, so Floyd just came by to check on me, to "Make sure yer still
alive!" as he says. No doubt Vicki sent him to find out if I was all good,
to see if they could do anything for me. Nova Scotian hospitality. It's a
real thing, and I love my adopted province for it. I assured him I'd be
gone by 11:00, even if the rain still lashed. I'm on borrowed time now.

The ferry I see crossing Grand Passage will soon be carrying a Dodge Grand Caravan full of the people I love: Genny, Rosalie, and Hazel, who turns ten years old *today*. My heart can barely hold on. And, after the hugs and tears, when I break down my bike, flip it upside down, and ratchet it to the roof rack, stuff my slew of wet stuff into the back, and slide the Tombstone home, I know this whole thing will be over.

There's something bittersweet about endings, isn't there? I know you know what I'm talking about. When you sailed into Fairhaven and slipped the *Spray* into her home berth, you thought your adventure was closing for good. You'd made it, you'd sailed around the world alone, you'd *lived* it. What, possibly, could ever compare to that?

But you had one more journey up your sleeve.

So this is goodbye, my friend. I'm going back to my family. I'm going back to the waves. In parting, I offer the words I found yesterday inscribed on the Slocum family pew in the Westport Baptist Church:

> *Not in the churchyard shall he sleep,*
> *Amid the silent gloom,*
> *His home was on the mighty deep,*
> *And there shall be his tomb.*

> *He loved his own bright, deep blue sea,*
> *O'er it he loved to roam,*
> *And now his winding sheet shall be,*
> *That same bright ocean's foam.*

> *No village bell shall toll for him,*
> *Its mournful, solemn dirge,*
> *The winds shall chant a requiem,*
> *To him beneath the surge.*

Peace out, my righteous dude. With love and gratitude,

RC

A Note of Gratitude

Without friends, solitude loses its sweetness. My heartfelt thanks to those whose curiosity and support buoyed me up along the way: Craig Rowe, Aaron Williams, Dan Boyce, Tania Wong, Kyle Knight, Melissa Bond, Ally Read, Ben Hawkins, Shelley Thomas, Matt Howard, Rob Chambers, Gillian Turnbull, and Ben Gibson.

Once I was at sea, the crew at Goose Lane Editions took great care of me. Simon Thibault challenged and championed in equal measure. James Langer brought an astute editorial eye and helped me find my line. Paula Sarson gave a masterclass in prose tightening. To these three experts — and to everyone at the Goose — I offer my sincere thanks.

To those who endorsed this expedition personally, I give bear hugs: Will Ferguson, Kate Inglis, James Mullinger, Tyler Leblanc, Chas Smith, and, especially, Afie Jurvanen. Thank you all.

And how can a voyage happen without a peerless craftsman and a crack cartographer? Special thanks to both Tony Ortolani for shaping the Tombstone, and Jeff Domm for forging the map.

My respect and reverence goes to Stan Grayson, author of *A Man for All Oceans*. If not for his incredible account of Joshua Slocum's life and legacy, my vessel would have sprung a leak years ago.

To my whole extended family, I send love and gratitude. I kept this one tight to the vest, but Bob and Terry Shaw's early vote of confidence meant the world. To Hazel and Rosalie, my kind and beautiful daughters, I thank you for the love you give right back. And then there's Genny. I am eternally grateful for your support and encouragement. You are everything to me. My fire will always burn for you.

Finally, to the province of Nova Scotia and its fine folks, I extend my humble gratitude. Thank you to everyone who welcomed my ragged flag on the road from Cow Bay to Brier Island. I continue to be amazed at the generosity I experienced along our stunning coastline. It is your stories that fill these sails.

A Note on Sources

Three sun-bleached and beat-up books were crucial to the genesis of this story. These are the editions I carried with me: *Rockbound* by Frank Parker Day (Toronto: University of Toronto Press, 1989); *Bluenose Ghosts* by Helen Creighton (Halifax: Nimbus Publishing, 1994); and *Sailing Alone Around the World* by Joshua Slocum (Boston: Shambhala Pocket Classics, 1999).

I drew inspiration and quotations from a number of other texts, including, in the order they appear in this book, *Harry Potter and the Half-Blood Prince* by J.K. Rowling (New York: Bloomsbury Children's Books, 2014); *The Doors of Perception* by Aldous Huxley (New York: Harper Perennial Modern Classics, 2009); *The Voyage of The Beagle* by Charles Darwin (New York: Penguin Classics, 1989); *How to Change Your Mind* by Michael Pollan (New York: Penguin Books, 2019); *The Essential Guide to the Tarot* by David Fontana (London: Watkins Publishing, 2011); and *A Man for All Oceans* by Stan Grayson (Massachusetts: Tilbury House, 2017).

RC Shaw is the author of *Captain Solitude* and *Louisbourg or Bust*, a finalist for the Margaret and John Savage First Book Award for Non-Fiction. He has written for the *Globe and Mail*, the *Surfer's Journal*, *[EDIT]*, *Beach Grit*, the *Coast*, and the *Chronicle Herald*. He also founded the Cow Bay Concert Series, bringing musical acts such as Bahamas, Matt Mays, and Jenn Grant to his community hall. He holds an MFA in Creative Non-Fiction from King's University College.

When not teaching high school English, RC Shaw can be found in the waves near his home in Cow Bay, Nova Scotia. He yearns to sail, but reading a dozen sailing books is the extent of his experience. He plans to enroll in a 'Learn to Sail' summer camp in the near future, likely alongside his pre-teen daughters.